December 1993

Win and C

I hope you
enjoy this entertaining
look at Hong Kong life!

With best wishes,

James

The Fragrant Chinese

The Fragrant Chinese

Anthony Lawrence

The Chinese University Press

Acknowledgements
The publisher would like to thank the following individuals
and organizations for their kind permission to reproduce the
photographs and comics in this book.

Photographs :
Courtesy of Hong Kong Government 2–3, 5, 8–9, 10–
11, 13, 15, 21, 56–57, 61, 64, 66, 109, 119, 122–123,
127, 136–137, 139, 140, 143, 146, 148–149, 151, 153,
154, 155, 157, 159, 181, 185, 198–199, 204–205, 207,
209, 210, 222–223, 225, 226, 227, 229; Hong Kong
Tourist Association 105, 174, 197; Xinhua News
Agency 36–37, 114–115; Chinese Opera Research
Project, The Chinese University of Hong Kong, 160–
161, 163, 165, 167, 169; Cheung Chan-fai 92–93, 94,
95, 97, 99, 100, 101; Albert Fung 70–71, 73, 74, 81, 82.

Comics :
Chi-kwan Chiu 31, 39, 51, 59, 91, 131, 180.

ISBN 962–201–572–7

THE CHINESE UNIVERSITY PRESS
The Chinese University of Hong Kong
SHATIN, N.T., HONG KONG

Printed in Hong Kong

Contents

Preface

My friend, T. L. Tsim, journalist, commentator, broadcaster and director of The Chinese University Press, told me over lunch one day that it was time I wrote a book on Chinese etiquette. When I protested that I knew nothing about etiquette, Chinese or any other kind, he brushed this impatiently aside. As I had lived and worked in the area for thirty-seven years and known many Chinese people, he said, there was no excuse for not writing about them. So this book was born. A radio and TV journalist trying to write a book is a piteous spectacle, like a man used to the hundred metres dash facing a ten mile marathon; yet trying to explain the attitudes of Chinese people has been a very important experience. If I learned anything at all, it is the difficulty, as Proust has insisted, of ever really knowing and understanding another human being. But the attempt is always worthwhile.

Many people helped in making this book. Kingsley Ma, production manager of The Chinese University Press, directed the art and design; Chi-kwan Chiu drew the comics; Michael Leung, of The Chinese University Press, took excellent photographs, as did Ricky Wong and Albert Fung. Mike Chung, graphic designer of The Chinese University Press, designed the book's cover and layout. Cheung Chan-fai, of the Department of Philosophy at The Chinese University of Hong Kong, allowed the use of his transparencies for the chapter on death and funerals. Grateful acknowlegements are also due to Sau Y. Chan, of the Department of Music at the same university, for his advice on Cantonese opera and for helping me secure permission from the Chinese Opera Research Project of the Department of Music at The Chinese University of Hong Kong to use the transparencies in the chapter on Cantonese opera.

I am particularly grateful for the interview granted me by the well-known opera stars Long Kim-sang and Mei Suet-shi who gave me a new appreciation of opera and the achievement of the Chor Fung Ming Troupe.

The Hong Kong Government Information Services and the Hong Kong Tourist Association provided transparencies; the New China News Agency (Xinhua) allowed use of photographs of the Shenzhen Special Economic Zone and Guangzhou.

Asking the opinions of Chinese friends in writing this book was an exhilarating experience. Hong Kong is a place of disconcerting variety, and one man's firm convictions are another's definition of old wives' bedtime stories. My wife, Irmgard, who knows far more Chinese language than I do, patiently read through the text. T. L. Tsim and other Chinese friends, notably Y. K. Fung and Kin-wai Wong, gave me their valued opinions. To avoid embarrassment I have had to omit the names of many admirable people whose ideas and utterances have enriched the record. Needless to say, any errors in this book must be laid at the door of the author.

Anthony Lawrence

Chapter 1

Here, Now

In four years from now Hong Kong will be very different from the place we know.

British colonial administration will have gone. Another regime will have taken over, with a Chief Executive approved by Beijing and important decisions in the hands of Mainland officials.

These coming changes cast long shadows. There's a feeling in the air of time running short, an urgent need for personal and family decisions.

The drive to make money is growing more feverish. Energetic men

After the Tiananmen crackdown of June,1989, Hong Kong demonstrators marched to Kai Tak airport, appealing to would-be emigrants to stay and defend their way of life.

exploit the cheap labour across the border and invest the big profits in short-term speculation, to beat the ten per cent inflation rate. Soaring flat prices and rents give you the chance to make a couple more fortunes before the fatal date of 1997. Contradictions abound. Social services are inadequate and the old and handicapped neglected, but so many Chinese you meet (especially the young and vigorous) are loud in praise of Hong Kong—the most convenient place in the world for daily living, "because everything is here".

How rapidly the kaleidoscope shifts! Let's take a look.

Now is the time to stop the television camera and recorder for a short break, give the tapes a quick going-over, put together a picture of Hong Kong people in this strange year of 1993. Not an easy script—the facts and human reactions need reassessing every couple of pages. So many interpretations—by leaders in Beijing trying to combine political dictatorship with economic freedom; by a new Governor with a new style; by businessmen and Hong Kong politicians; by social reformers. If not recorded now, too much will be forgotten.

The handover of Britain's last sizeable colony will be against the wishes of most of the close-on-six-million people living here; but nothing can stop it. What imprint will today's Hong Kong leave on the future Special Administrative Zone? What customs and attitudes will change or disappear?

A man who had lived in Hong Kong for thirty years said: "Never try explaining this place to outsiders. They're almost bound to suspect you of being paid by the Government to do a public relations job."

It is true, fate has given Hong Kong an extraordinarily favourable deal. It was on the China Mainland that the Communists, in the early days of the great Maoist experiments, would claim they were creating a new kind of human being, a selfless idealist, an example to the developing world. That never happened. Instead it's been Hong Kong without great leadership or any coherent declared philosophy, which has produced a new kind of Chinese man and woman. It's an amalgam—a Chinese personality sculpted by thousands of years of history but altered and modified by non-Chinese influences. The process has taken a long time to develop, but now the local scene is enlivened by a cast of unusual characters more energetic, courageous and articulate than the Chinese on the Mainland or in Taiwan or Singapore. They make use of

Young audiences attend a concert in aid of the June 1989 student movement on the Mainland.

Hong Kong's freedom to comment sharply on the local scene. And what a scene! The great airport scheme; Governor Patten's proposals for constitutional changes and the fury he's aroused from across the Border: the Harbour filling with sewage; ever-soaring rents.

Hong Kong is a far livelier place than it was even ten years ago. And the years ahead promise more chapters of the unexpected. The whole world is changing so rapidly and these changes—the collapse of world communism, the death of aging Chinese leaders and the Mainland drive towards a more open economy—all this will affect Hong Kong and the people here to an extent we can only guess at.

Meanwhile the Hong Kong people who will live through these changes are all around us today, acting out their lives, developing points of view, modifying prejudices, planning their children's future. They are the raw material of history by which reputations will stand or fall.

During thirty odd years in Hong Kong I have come to know many Chinese people, but sometimes a long stay has to be paid for in unexpected ways. Objectivity may suffer. In his first months and years the newcomer makes great efforts to find out everything he can about the local scene and after two years or so may feel he is reasonably knowledgeable, that he more or less knows it all. Then the scene has greatly changed but he goes on thinking in the old way, mouthing old impressions, though some of his ideas are out-of-date by now; and his generalizations about Chinese attitudes too often risk hearty laughter from the young.

It has been refreshing to be updated by Hong Kong friends and acquaintances in the course of recent research. I was surprised to find how peoples' thinking has changed. Life holds far more variety than even ten years ago, and young people have been very quick to enjoy new-found freedoms. Hong Kong remains very Chinese and down-to-earth but how vigorously it has adopted certain Western elements of living! The very uncertainty of the years ahead, it may be, has made young people more flexible in their attitudes; they look around more than they did for anything helpful to success and financial security. Five thousand years of continuous civilization can still be relied on to provide many answers but good qualifications and the sophistication of the world (as well as good connections) may be more effective still.

A Western journalist's picture of Hong Kong attitudes and behaviour in 1993 cannot hope to be more than a series of impressions, derived from contacts and conversations, some with friends of long standing, some with strangers. Yet never mind its limitations, it can still serve a human purpose—

The Communist insurance company's advertisement on a tram says, "Our guarantees are as hard as steel."

鐵一般保障

WESTERN MARKET
市街環上

中國保險公司香港分

of perhaps helping Hong Kong people to understand each other better. In Hong Kong the expatriates usually know very little about the local Chinese. This is roughly equalled by the ignorance of local Chinese about the expatriate or even sometimes about their own people.

The Hong Kong Chinese world is not one community—to some it appears more like a vast and very peculiar transit camp frequented by all kinds of strangers. There are Chinese here who feel more at ease with foreigners than they do with their own countrymen; Chinese from two adjoining Mainland counties who can't understand each other's speech and follow differing customs. In some ways, the gap between the villager out in the countryside

P.A.D.S.—the new Port and Airport Development Scheme is a big issue in the London-Hong Kong-Beijing confrontation. The large model of the airport at Chek Lap Kok was shown to Mainland experts but Beijing was unimpressed.

tending the vegetables and the big-time Stock Exchange operator is very wide—wider than that between a Chinese university teacher, journalist or government servant and his European counterpart.

Yet Chineseness goes deep, and out of all this human variety it's a confidently eager yet shrewdly appraising Chinese face which emerges. The way the Chinese play the game of life in Hong Kong has many lessons for the rest, the Westerners, the people from outside, about staying human and even prospering in a sometimes nightmare world.

Chapter 2

Pride, Prejudice and Pleasant Surprises

The Chinese are certainly different from Westerners and find plenty of historical reasons for disliking them. There's a special need for caution, they have often thought, when dealing with the British.

The story of Sino-British relations makes embarrassing reading for everyone concerned. Such a futile inventory of decades of unhappy encounters — Opium Wars; ruthless exploitation of China's material wealth and technological backwardness; overzealous and presuming missionaries; boundless imperial dignity without weapons to back it up; conflicting ideas about propriety, virtue and trade.

It used to be said that Hong Kong people were non-political, interested only in money and food. Yet when students and workers were fired on in Beijing's Tiananmen area in June, 1989, a million Hong Kong people demonstrated in protest.

All that belongs to the past, you may say; yet even today many Western views of the Chinese are based on stories of Chinese cunning and deviousness; and the Chinese, although few of them regard the Westerners as especially clever, often feel they would prefer to dispense with their presence, because in the Chinese universe they are not really necessary — apart from certain of their technological skills.

However some Chinese, especially the better educated ones, have come to admit, reluctantly, that they are not necessarily the vital core of the earth's inhabitants. True, close on a quarter of humans are Chinese, but they really are outnumbered even though forming a great human mass of twelve hundred million. And as they strive and multiply in the middle of the Far East, one of the most striking and tragic aspects of this scene is the failure of the Chinese and the rest of the human race to come together — understand each other and communicate to mutual benefit.

Tragic, because through ignorance of Chinese history, art, literature and philosophy the outside world is deprived of a huge reservoir of human wisdom and experience. And because of China's abiding prejudices and complexes where the West is concerned a billion people culturally stagnate in the Third World instead of assuming their necessary role as the leading power in developing Asia. The Communists aimed at changing this but their vista was limited to asserting China's place in the sun without increasing understanding of the rest of the world. So they have failed, defeated by the very Chineseness of China — its harking back to the past and distrust of the foreigner.

Nevertheless there are many people in the Western world who take a positive view of China, and this is not just an affair of left-wingers approving what they imagine to be Communist purity. Many Westerners retain a vague idea of the Chinese as a cheerful, hardworking, family-oriented people surviving indomitably floods, earthquakes and wartime atrocities. Western intellectuals, after mastering the difficulties of Chinese language and penetrating the forests of the Tang, Song or Ching dynasties, often develop a kind of proprietorial interest, and write as if they were experts; which of course nobody can be where China is concerned, there is simply too much of it.

Better not love or patronize the Chinese. In the last hundred years scores

Small operators use the Hong Kong Stock Exchange like a gambling casino. Boom times bring in the lucky dollars.

of intelligent outsiders (missionary doctors, educators, engineers) have come from the West to help modernize China. These efforts have often ended in misunderstanding and eventual failure because the Chinese were suspicious of their motives. They were seen as power-seeking, tainted by espionage or, at the least, threatening traditional ways of doing things.

Yet, as growing numbers of people in both worlds will tell you, when barriers are breached, misunderstandings dissolved and friendships finally consolidated, the results can be quite extraordinary and the rewards more lasting than could ever have been expected. This can happen when reasonable individuals, laying aside for a while the warnings of history and ancestors, take strangers as they find them.

Many people with Chinese acquaintance will tell you that first introductions and encounters are usually agreeable, because the Chinese are by nature polite and hospitable and go to great lengths to make guests feel at ease. It's the interim stages that are difficult.

If Westerners are going to understand Chinese people, both in Hong Kong and on the Mainland, they will have to know something about Confucius — Kong zi. This is the sage who lived in the sixth century B.C., suffered more disappointments than usually fall to the lot of wise men, and died feeling his life had been largely wasted.

Personal sayings of Kong zi take up only a few slim volumes; the interpretations by disciples and commentators fill a library; but the essential precepts of this great social philosopher have echoed down the centuries, and however much the modern world has changed, his sayings are still repeated in Chinese communities and children are brought up on them.

"Be careful not to exaggerate the point," says a friendly Hong Kong Chinese journalist. "The kind of rich, Westernized people you're likely to meet in Hong Kong won't admit to much connection with Confucius. As for the masses, they are too busy looking after the family rice bowl to worry about philosophy."

He speaks only a half truth. The very rich are a small minority, fascinating but unrepresentative. Most Hong Kong Chinese are in the world of ups and downs, in small-sized apartments, New Territories villages, and especially in the labyrinths of the Hong Kong housing estates. Here a Chinese human tide flows and swirls in lively intercourse and strictly confined space; and without careful attention to behaviour and social routines, daily existence there would be impossible. They rely on Confucian rules of decent conduct often without realizing it.

Confucius put great store on filial piety. "The superior man, while his parents are alive, reverently nourishes them." This is not taken lightly. Most Hong Kong people give anything between a tenth and a third of their take-home pay to the parents. The philosopher also says that "rulers should cultivate their own characters and honour men of virtue and talent; and deal with the mass of the people as children. The citizen with an upright heart controls his family; families being regulated, the state is rightly governed. The states being rightly governed, the whole kingdom is made tranquil and happy."

Christmas decorations in Tsimshatsui. Christians are few in Hong Kong but people enjoy the lights and the sales and the present-giving.

Confucius also laid down the duties of women. He enjoined a state of subservience to mothers-in-law and husbands. This would today sound strangely in the ears of a smart, Westernized, Hong Kong girl. Yet she would be aware of the tradition. You may argue that all great religions and social philosophies are working towards the same human and moral objectives, but in their respect for parents and elders the Chinese leave Westerners rather far behind.

Apart from this there's a general emphasis on personal virtue. Many Chinese people, when they talk about improving life and the way the place is run, are less interested in changes in institutions than in finding honest administrators. "When the Communists took over China in 1949," said a former Mainland teacher, "we all respected them because they shared our conditions and lived modestly like the people. When they began driving about in big cars with curtains over the windows, then we lost faith. We need men of high integrity, never mind the system."

"I didn't actually read the Confucian analects when I was small," a young shop assistant will admit. "But I was taught how to behave by my parents and grandparents — you know, respect for teachers, love of parents and family, love of friends — all of that. It was often not what my parents actually said. I saw them behaving with kindness and respect towards their own parents, and so it seemed to me that this was what everyone should do. Of course schoolteachers reinforce this and, though you may not believe it, I learned quite a lot of morality from films — no, I'm not joking; the good people always seemed so much more attractive than the nasty ones."

Often in China's modern history Confucian teaching, with its emphasis on personal virtue and self-control and its lack of interest in such material matters as industry, science and weapons of destruction, has been seen as an obstacle to national progress. In the early days of the Nationalist Party, the KMT, Chiang Kai-shek tried to push it all to one side, but he was obliged to bring it back later. The Communists ran national campaigns against it. Yet, whether they read Confucius or not, Chinese peoples' conduct remains Confucius-influenced — rather as Western agnostics and atheists may reject Holy Writ but nonetheless order their day-to-day conduct as if it were still the embodiment of truth.

You might well say that Confucian thinking in Hong Kong is especially modified by all the varying influences and pressures of the world outside. That is also true of part of the Mainland. Modern town life was unknown to the great teacher. Sheer lack of living space makes it impossible for young marrieds to obey the Confucian principle that they should stay with the man's parents as long as they live. Hong Kong wives are less obedient to their mothers-in-law.

We're So Terrific

Hong Kong is a unique human harbour, half-choked with self-congratulatory *clichés*. Some of them are even true. Men do come here to make money in a free atmosphere and some succeed brilliantly. The food really is wonderful and taxes are low. In such waters all kinds of human craft find mooring. A Chinese newspaper described it as a "Wuhuabamen de shehui" a five flowers eight doors sort of society, meaning thoroughly strange and mixed up. How many important injections, additives and modifications have its inhabitants suffered and absorbed?

Not even Hong Kong's weather holds them back. For half the year, from May to October, long hot, wet summer months would encourage sloth, siesta and general lassitude in any other tropical city, but not here. Men actually wear suits in the noonday.

The dynamism of the place expresses a certain recklessness. "Don't just open a barber's shop," advised a man leaving college. "Open a chain of them with a manager for each. Get the money from the bank. Just get on with it."

"People in Hong Kong like to launch their own businesses," says a young woman planning to do just that. "It is so easy to start up. The registration process is cheap and simple. And then, if you've begun with a really good idea and luck turns your way, hard work can bring good rewards. If you just slog along for somebody else you're like the character for work — "gong" (工) you're the middle stroke that never manages to stick out at the top. Whereas, if you're on your own and you hit the jackpot … Waaa!"

Southern Chinese (this includes Hong Kongers) invite comparison with

Southern Italians. Hong Kongers are passionate, lively, enjoy eating and suffer the extortion of Mafia-type secret societies, they also work hard, and this is the theme of many after dinner speeches — this special get-up-and-go quality of the Hong Kong workforce. Actually the people have little choice; if a family doesn't look after itself the prospects are grim. There is no welfare state to cushion the blows of fate. So people do indeed work very hard, and spend much of their earnings on good, nourishing food, finding relaxation in gambling and the enjoyment of festivals and anniversaries, combining in formidable family groups to stave off disaster and make dreams come true. They are a luxuriant, successful growth in a jungle of conflicting moral and material forces. The four hundred or so square miles of Hong Kong are at once the scene of a colonial afterglow; capitalism red in tooth and claw; inexplicable public generosity (they will rake up twenty million dollars to feed hungry children in a country they've never heard of before); and movements dedicated to ideas of democracy unknown in China's five thousand years of continuous history. They read mass circulation cartoons of violence, indulge in disco and *karaoke* bars. The wicked are fearsome and the virtuous sometimes totally admirable, rather as in Dickens' earlier novels. There are naughty schoolgirls augmenting their pocket money with discreet prostitution but also teenage heroines holding a family together by bringing up small brothers and sisters. And as a background to it all a readiness to emigrate and start life again in a new country if this will help the family survive and prosper.

People from North China are quieter, less excitable. Of course all Chinese look alike to the Western newcomers, just as all Westerners look and sound alike to the Chinese. Especially they confuse the English spoken by English and Australians, although North American is more easily identified.

When Westerners first arrive out here, the Chinese they meet may be rather untypical. Unlike the mass of people on the Mainland (who know no foreigners all their lives) they will be used to foreign contacts because of work and business.

These Westernized Chinese are used to the odd behaviour and general ignorance on the part of newcomers from Britain, Europe, America and Australasia and are delightfully informal and easy going. None of the ceremo-

Housing-estate life for a teenager can be dull. Some find escape in the books of cartoon violence.

nious phrases of their grandfathers' times when a Chinese man, introduced to another, would murmur: "*Jiuyang! Jiuyang!*" (I have long held up your name for admiration). Older men may still ask to know another's "honourable name" and old-style politeness demands the answer: "My lowly name is Chan" (or whatever).

The younger generation has none of this. There was a time when an educated Chinese was steeped in his country's classical literature, and conversation was enlivened by quotations at once understood by the similarly well-read. Nowadays very few people in Hong Kong have received an old-style education in the classics and the man who lards his talk with quotations is considered affected as well as incomprehensible. However the pendulum swings and interest in Chinese literature is reported to be reviving, with more and more Hong Kong people able to speak Mandarin. A visitor from Beijing was heard to say recently that literary phrases are now heard more often there.

The Western newcomer is unconcerned with all this, as he can speak only English with his Chinese acquaintance; and in this medium what counts is a general attitude of interest and goodwill — as well as a knowledge of certain minor procedures, such as using both hands to proffer a name-card, or money. Money is better slipped into an envelope — a red envelope if you're doing someone a favour.

At a dinner points are scored when Western guests say how much they enjoy Chinese food, especially what is on that evening's menu, and wish to know more about Chinese customs.

Like most people, the Chinese appreciate praise of their way of life despite their laughingly modest disclaimers. In private they admit to a feeling of pride at belonging to the longest continuous civilization on earth. Nevertheless they are keenly aware that, for various regrettable reasons, this great civilization did fall badly behind during the last century or so, even though they suspect the main cause was only the temporary advantage enjoyed by Westerners in technology and automatic weapons. So it does give pleasure when outsiders express admiration for the achievements of China's past, confidence in the future, and respect for China's culture in general. However don't overdo it. Your hosts are pretty well informed about the Cultural Revolution and other recent horrors in their great country's story.

Differences, Suspicions and Confidence

Chinese people in Hong Kong and on the Mainland differ profoundly not only according to age but also in place of origin, personal and family wealth, education, and connections. A specially decisive factor is the amount and quality of contacts with the world outside. The Mainland also has links but these are relatively fewer, more difficult to come by and the more eagerly sought. Relatively fewer young Mainlanders study abroad. Of that lucky few, many never return. Those that do tend to be the reformers, supporters of change.

The 1989 demonstration of sympathy with the Mainland student was completely orderly. But Hong Kong has never been the same since.

In Hong Kong there's virtually unrestricted coming and going. Life effervesces with new ideas of culture, new thinking. Men from a traditional background seek to adapt to a world unknown to Kong zi. Lively products of Wellesley or M.I.T. return to regard old-fashioned parents as amusing dinosaurs (while taking care to mind their respectful manners).

The Northern Chinese call the Westerners "*yangren*," meaning those who come from across the ocean. When they want to be insulting they call the foreigners "*yangguizi*," that means ocean ghosts. The Cantonese Chinese call the Westerners "*gweilos*," that means foreign devils or foreign ghosts, but now the foreigners have begun using the phrase to describe themselves and polite Chinese will assure you there is nothing contemptuous in its meaning, it simply suggests a "non-person" — a non-Chinese. Sometimes it's explained that "foreign ghost" is only a harmless reaction to Westerners' pale faces. Other Chinese will admit that "gweilo" is still a rather disagreeable name to call anyone. It has little to do with old unhappy confrontation but much more with Chinese dismay at the hairiness of Western hands and arms, the length of nose, the smell on hot days, the occasional profusion of beard. Within living memory Chinese children, on seeing a Western man, would run screaming in fear to their mothers' arms.

There is this saying about skin-colour — how the divine Master Baker made the human race, and the first batch he took from the oven had been in there too long — they came out black. With the second batch he went too far the other way and they were all too pale. But the third time he got it right and out came his prize-winning achievement — the Yellow Race.

Chinese are sensitive; so are Westerners; though the mental voltage is different. In the first social exchange, even your sophisticated Chinese executive may well be shocked (although he won't show it) if he's asked direct, searching questions about his political opinions by a visitor with a probing mind.

"I think it might be a good idea," said a Chinese fellow guest after a dinner, "if you avoided too much interrogation. It's better just to keep the conversation going and you will learn things sooner or later — indirectly, by a sort of mental osmosis. It may take some months but it is better that way."

Which is no great consolation to a journalist whose editor wanted the feature story yesterday. This kindly critic really meant to be helpful. He belonged to a generation grown up and matured on the Mainland of the old days and he had brought the atmosphere of his youth to restless, everchanging Hong Kong. Though their numbers are dwindling there are many like him.

Yet the Westerner may also suffer embarrassment. The Chinese is shocked to be asked at first encounter about his political views. The Westerner may be taken aback to be asked how old he and his wife are, how much salary they earn and how much they pay for their flat. That isn't at all rude by Chinese standards; it simply shows an intelligent friendly interest. After all, you can always answer evasively, with the self-excusing laugh so helpful to Chinese-style exchanges.

It used to be said that every Chinese felt himself to be superior to all other races. Even the man sweeping the gutter and splashed by the mud of the passing foreigner's Rolls Royce could feel as he cursed: "At least I am not one of them. At least I am Chinese."

Now your Chinese acquaintance will disavow any such views. "We don't feel ourselves so superior but," he will add with an enigmatic smile, "we do feel ourselves to be different."

Today contradictions flourish in the same Chinese family, even in the heart of the same Chinese man or woman. Making use of an alert intelligence they strike a careful balance between tradition and contemporary realities. Some businessmen, despite their expensively-cut suits and American or clipped British accents, use a very non-Western approach when planning the launch of a hundred-million-dollar joint venture or take-over bid. An autocratic patriarch in the background may be making the real decisions. Father is calling the tune; filial obedience is decisive.

And a commercial big-shot, though he mingles with the establishment, frequents Western clubs and shows all outward signs of shedding his origins, will still want his family around him at New Year, will still observe respect for ancestors, consult fortune-tellers, hire *feng shui* (geomancy) experts when choosing a new office.

Twenty years ago Westerners in Hong Kong, especially the British, still looked down on the local Chinese, who found this attitude utterly insulting. Yet there was nothing especially anti-Chinese about this. The British looked down on everybody. If a foreigner seemed not to understand a perfectly simple English request or order it was just repeated more loudly. The Chinese would react to this by assuming a mask of icy disapproval, as if encountering an unpleasant smell from drains. This is how they acquired a reputation of always looking inscrutable.

How everything has changed! Pointless, nowadays, to try making a cartoon caricature of the arrogant British abroad. The model has ceased to exist. The impenetrable armour of English southern accent and what used to be Oxbridge manner is virtually obsolete.

This is partly related to the dissolution of the British Empire, partly to the downgrading of a whole social layer by the lives and times of the pro-Soviet agents — Philby and the rest. The British themselves often don't realize how the misdeeds of these men changed foreign attitudes towards Britain's conventions and famous institutions.

Yet it is a fact that individuals and nations who have come down in the world tend to be more agreeable company than those on the way up or calling the shots from the top. Britain still runs Hong Kong but without the former colonial-economic muscle; and this makes it easier for British and Chinese to meet on socially equal terms. There are so many more Chinese millionaires and billionaires, so much Japanese, American and China Mainland investment. All of this has modified the impact of the British presence and made attitudes more relaxed.

Not that the Hong Kong Chinese have ever protested strongly over their inferior colonial status. Nor by any means have all the British serving the colonial government in Hong Kong maintained a pompous isolation. Some have identified themselves closely with Hong Kong people and problems; cut red tape, won respect, held the ring, so to speak, to enable local energy and initiative to create the wealth; and they have left many friends behind when they went home.

Another cause for colonialism's acceptance here lies in Chinese psychology — something we have possibly noticed in the host at even the first social

A bar on Lan Kwai Fong. Soft lights, friendly atmosphere.

get-together — a deeply rooted obsession with easy relationships and harmony, avoidance of confrontation. You may think, listening to two Hong
Kong people talking loudly, that they are well into an all-out stand up slanging
match; only when they suddenly burst out laughing do you realize this isn't a
row at all — it's just that Cantonese sounds like that. Chinese people have the
admirable quality of wanting everyone around them to be happy and contented, and they carry this rather far. Exceptions are few.

The principle of non-confrontation exerts a deep influence on politics,
encouraging passive attitudes; and it shows itself even more in the conduct of
daily life. Queueing at a local bus stop one Sunday afternoon a Western
woman realized, after waiting twice the usual fifteen minutes, that the service
had been discontinued without warning. To a group of Chinese girls next to
her she declared: "This so-and-so bus company has stopped its Sunday service
without telling anyone. Let's all protest. I'll send them a strong letter, and you
do the same."

The girls smiled, shook their heads. Thank you, but no. "Do you always
complain about things?" one of them asked. "We never do."

"It is true," said a Cantonese teacher. "We prefer to put up with what we've got. We think of that Confucian precept about a man first controlling himself and his family before worrying about affairs of state. We feel ourselves, most of the time, to be concerned with that first stage, concentrating on family problems."

A young businessman disagreed. "Nothing whatever to do with Confucius. It is simply that we Chinese have been influenced by centuries of uncertainty, unpredictable government and unexpected catastrophe. So we study very closely the business of survival. Why speak out and protest? The individual opinion will probably at best be ignored; and it might even land you in trouble. You may say the chances of that happening in Hong Kong are a thousand to one against, but why risk it? Your name gets on a list and before you know where you are there's a file on you in some office."

Small voter turnouts and even smaller party registration have sometimes been the political effect of this attitude. The middle-aged, the bourgeois, those with the traditional outlook, prefer to put up with whatever government is in power, rather than get involved in some group requiring them to stand up and voice their opposition in public. They submit to authority, like the simple millions of farmers on the China Mainland, suffering their village bosses and the graft and corruption, hoping only that virtuous officials may appear from nowhere and clean things up.

Are attitudes changing? Of course they are, faster in Hong Kong than across the border. Despite stern warnings from the Communists nearly forty per cent (and possibly fifty per cent) of voters turned out at the 1991 Hong Kong elections. They could hope for anonymity because the ballot was secret. Still, it showed a new interest in the political scene, as if Hong Kong were reflecting a worldwide restless movement on the part of an emerging middle class less and less prepared to put up with dictatorship without having its voice heard.

Who would ever have thought the 1989 democracy movement in Beijing would have so stirred the allegedly non-political Hong Kong citizens? Who would have imagined the summer demonstration when nearly a million people — a sixth of the entire Hong Kong population — took to the streets? That came as a surprise to everyone, to officialdom, the police, political commentators, to the old men in Beijing, even to those taking part in the peaceful protest march.

At later demonstrations, when the television cameras were focussing more closely on the crowds, the numbers dwindled.

Not all Chinese are frightened of confrontation. China past and present has its martyrs to truth, dissidents, revolutionaries (women as well as men), honest ministers rebuking emperors well-knowing what it would cost them. But until now they have always been a small minority.

Chinese change when they get away from China. In a different atmosphere they transform themselves into outspoken Americans or Australians; and raise their voices. A Hong Kong woman visiting family in Boston was amazed by the behaviour of her American-naturalized sister. "She gave the restaurant people hell because the meat was cooked wrong and heads were turning at the noise. In Hong Kong we wouldn't dream of doing that. We'd keep our voices down, simply never eat in that place again."

All these ingredients, mixed in varying proportions, make a very human Chinese drama with five and three quarter million actors, and some of the roles are disconcerting, to say the least. A materialistic surface covers the customs, etiquette, superstitions, the accumulated experience of scores of centuries. New generations are entering the stage bringing all kinds of ideas, some from the peoples and places they have visited or seen on TV, some worked out by themselves, some inherited and modified by use.

In Hong Kong, in this decade of transience and mental revolution, it's not surprising that many people hesitate and find it hard to make decisions.

"Half the people here raise a hearty cheer for a democrat leader like Martin Lee," said an office secretary, "and the other half wishes he would shut up because for them he's a dangerous element who will get everyone into trouble."

"More and more of the younger generation are saying we ought to have democracy. Though it's open to abuse it's the only way that really allows Hong Kong people to run Hong Kong. But if you're married with children are you going to be crazy enough to upset Beijing? Do you want a Tienanmen here in Hong Kong?"

Chapter 3

Questions of Face

Even before arrival in the Far East the newcomer will have heard or read about "face" — the need the Chinese feel for dignity and personal prestige to be upheld or, better still, enhanced. This is a touchy subject. Of course "face" is important, and not only if you're Chinese. Nowhere in the world do people relish being snubbed or carelessly insulted. Who doesn't like to be treated with respect?

Yet face with the Chinese is something at once more and less

Lunch out of a paper rice-box if you're in a hurry or want to save money; but you lose face if your rich friends pass by and see you.

vital to mental comfort. Its ingredients include a hidden desire to show off and impress the neighbours. You give a man face when you help him feel and appear more important than he really is. You lose face when you are revealed as a would-be big shot who hasn't quite made it.

Things become more sensitive when people who know they belong to the oldest continuous civilization in the world are in close contact with another race enjoying a superior position which, as most Chinese are convinced, their culture doesn't really entitle them to. Of course nobody would say that these non-Chinese people are actually barbarians, but certainly they seem to have been enjoying unfair temporary advantages because of certain lucky technical discoveries, rather than their moral or intellectual qualities.

Quite apart from foreign contacts the Chinese people of Hong Kong have enough to do looking after face among their own compatriots. Face has so much to do with self-respect and also the respect of those around you — friends, office colleagues, neighbours, the police, competitors in the battle of life. You lose face whenever something happens (whether through your own fault or not) which means a failure of your influence, power or prestige. Loss of face may be advanced as the reason for objecting to carrying out an order or doing a favour. "I am sorry, that is impossible, I should lose face."

Face at Work
Some Western bosses in Hong Kong upset their staff without even meaning to. Some are far more considerate and overpolite than they need to be. The solution, as in most human relationships, is civilized, commonsense behaviour (though don't be surprised if, once in a while, you meet a sudden, unexplained resistance to what seemed at the time a reasonable request).

If in the office a subordinate makes a mistake, never upbraid him before his colleagues; if you do he will want to murder you. Take him on one side and do it quietly. If, in a flash of cunning, you publicly praise him and his work and then follow with the private ticking-off, this shows in you a real talent for oriental man-management.

The late F. D. Ommanney in his *Fragrant Harbour* tells how back in 1945 a government official (a Westerner) thought his wristwatch had been stolen

and accused the Chinese servant who cleaned his bedroom. This was a poor, thin, little elderly man who had begged for the job, saying that he was starving, as indeed he seemed to be. The police were called in and questioned him, but he indignantly denied he had seen the watch. They were about to march him off to the police station when the watch was found. The government officer apologized and offered to make him a present of money to soothe his wounded pride. But the little man said with great and rather terrifying dignity: "I lose face because of you. I would rather starve than work for you." And he walked out of the house with the policemen.

However when a Chinese friend read over this chapter he expressed doubts. This was a story about pride rather than face, he thought. The servant had, if anything, actually been given face by the Westerner, who was apologizing and offering money; and the man had shown a reckless, absurd pride in refusing it. "In fact," said my critic, "I think Ommanney was told a made-up story."

Face can be related to the work you do. Certain jobs are considered to be "face-losing". You do not wish it to be generally known that your mother pushes dim sum trolleys around in a local restaurant. You don't want neighbours to see elderly members of your family calling the wares at a hawker's stall. Another sensitive area is old peoples' homes, some of which, despite all you hear, are comfortable and well-run. Nevertheless you tend to conceal the fact that you've shunted your grandparents into one of these establishments. Why? Hard to say, exactly. Something to do with the tradition (largely inapplicable to Hong Kong's crowded scene) that you stay with your parents so long as they live.

Face considerations decide quite large numbers of elderly Hong Kong people against claiming the old-age allowance. Hong Kong is the arena of individual effort and independence. You would lose face if people knew you were accepting that money from the Government.

Face affects Hong Kong politics. To be beaten in an election is an enormous loss of face, and because they don't want to risk the exposure of political in-fighting and the possible humiliations of defeat, many public figures in Hong Kong aren't prepared to contest a Legislative Council seat, even though they have given valuable service to Hong Kong when the Government called on them and placed them in some position of responsibility.

This is not just Hong Kong, it applies to China's painful Mainland experiments with representative government. The writer Shen Congwen's father left town and did not see his family again for twelve years after being defeated in elections to the Hunan Provincial Congress, the first to be held after the fall of the Manchus.

A Hong Kong businesswoman, prominent in public life, said two years ago: "The issue over direct elections is a real dilemma. Hong Kong people are still very prejudiced against direct elections. Our Confucian upbringing, which disciplines us to be modest and not fight for power, is still very deeply embedded.... A lot of good local people will not stand for elections. It's a question of face. They are too proud. They want to be appointed but do not have the guts to fight an election. It's a misfortune for Hong Kong that there are such people, even on the Legislative Council, who have that frame of mind."

As the businesswoman said, this is a real dilemma for Hong Kong people and it is advisable not to tease them about it. For their reply may well be

You lose face if you beg. Hong Kong people say you can always find some way to earn a living instead of begging.

something like: "The British never allowed us to play a part in local politics until very recently; and now they are dumping us. They retarded us politically and now they are letting us down. Their democratic proposals come too late."

The traditional Chinese view is this: To be appointed is to be invited to serve because of one's infinite wisdom and good judgment. To run for office is to covet political power. To the Chinese mind, the latter is the act of a charlatan. Ambition is not considered a virtue among the Chinese people and many do their best to hide it.

How rapidly the scene changes!

Social Life

Needless to say face is also a social question. A hostess said the worst loss of face is when you ask a friend to an important affair and she turns you down on a flimsy excuse. And you suffer agonies of loss of face when you ask important guests and, due to some mistake or incompetence by the cook, the food is well below standard. This could be one of the few occasions when your usually admirable Chinese friend would lose his temper at the waiters. People go to great lengths to avoid such predicaments — often spend money they can't afford.

"People in Hong Kong care too much about face," said a middle class housewife. "We know people who are spending eight thousand dollars a month on payments for a Benz, dressing beyond their means, inviting friends to meals at high-class hotels (and hoping they won't order much)."

Isn't this a universal phenomenon? Of course it is, but in Hong Kong the desire to succeed, to enjoy the good time, is more intense and feverish as 1997 approaches. There's a new interest in appearing to belong to the respectable bourgeois strata of society.

"The worst example of loss of face I can give you," said a university teacher, "is when a young man gets a respectable young girl in the family way. Leaving the girl out of it, it's a shocking loss of face for her parents that they failed to exercise efficient control to prevent such a catastrophe happening, and also for the parents of the boy, that they didn't raise him in a more civilized manner."

Face soaks into Hong Kong life in the oddest ways. "Look how the pawnshops here preserve the face of the customer," said a local reporter. "Not only the special screen inside the entrance so that you can't look in from the street, but once you're inside the assistant can't see your face, he's perched high up. Your anonymity's protected."

In teasing conversation among friends, a girl tells a young man to shut the window or get another chair from the bedroom; and the young man automatically replies, "If I follow your orders directly I'd be losing face." And sometimes, without knowing even what story they're quoting, the man in the street or the ferry will offer the excuse: "How can I possibly cross the Yangtze River and face the elders to the east with the story of my defeat?" It trips off the Chinese tongue without thinking, applied to any situation. The line just quoted refers actually to an incident two thousand years ago in China's history, when the great General Xiangyu was facing defeat at the hands of the new Han regime.

Chinese children know about face from an early age. Father likes to reprimand and discipline them in front of guests, to increase his feeling of importance. The guests and the children are quite aware of this and make allowances. Until recently children never dreamed of correcting or contradicting father. Only in the most careful and tactful way was it possible to suggest that there might conceivably be an alternative to the words of wisdom just fallen from his revered lips. However, like so many traditions in Hong Kong, this is changing. An independent-minded woman of thirty said: "I am amazed at the way children speak up nowadays and even tell father he's got it all wrong. It really is a generation gap."

The housewife is concerned with face in her own way. When friends are invited home to a meal she'll prepare more dishes than are needed, more than anyone could eat, to give an impression of wealth and abundance. When praised for the meal she says it's nothing, nothing. Hosts in restaurants after ordering a banquet, apologize for having done so badly, with such poor food and inadequate arrangements. A French-speaking Chinese diplomat did all this in a loud voice in a world-famous Paris restaurant. The restaurant sued him.

Chapter 4

Cantonese and Complications

"Don't be taken in by all that rags-to-riches bullshit about chaps arriving in Hong Kong with nothing and making billions in five years," says a Chinese lawyer friend. "You'll find that most of today's rich come from rich families. Hong Kong society has crystallized."

Yet a strong belief persists that with hard work and a bit of luck you can hit the jackpot here. And if you do manage the break-through, make it to the top or near it, how comfortable Hong Kong life can be in a luxury flat, with a car, holidays abroad, good education for the children. Even if you don't make a fortune life in Hong Kong does offer agreeable surroundings which make you very conscious of the gap separating conditions in many villages on the Mainland from even lower-middle-class living in Hong Kong.

Hong Kong prosperity has spread north across the border into Guangdong province and modernized the capital, Guangzhou. Highrise business blocks, luxury hotels, see new joint ventures, profits, good living.

A Hong Kong office manager said: "I am like thousands of others. When Chinese New Year comes round we visit the relatives my parents said goodbye to twenty years ago; and it's downright embarrassing."

How primitive they seem — and how demanding! "I shan't go next year," says a disgusted shop proprietor from North Point. "They were really ungrateful. A black-and-white TV wasn't good enough; they expected a colour set. I came back to Hong Kong wearing my nephew's clothes; they took the suit off my back as well as all the cash I could spare."

Yet such is the pace of change, stories like this no longer apply to many parts of Guangdong province. Deng Xiaoping's open door policy has brought money and comfort into countless homes. The Special Economic Zones have seen new businesses and factories starting up, new hotels, restaurants and shops selling smart clothes, watches, bicycles, tape-recorders, TV sets. The provincial capital, Guangzhou (Canton) has become a closer relation of Hong Kong, with something of its energy, emerging entrepreneurs, extortion rackets and call girls.

These changes have been developing for years; they're no longer so sensational. Less expected has been the prosperity of the Pearl River Delta and also the money flowing to upland villages used only to bare subsistence living.

"It takes your breath away," said a Hong Kong office worker after a visit to cousins in the Guangdong hills. "They are having new houses built now, they have carpets on the floor, they eat meat as often as they like — they are better off than we are in Hong Kong!"

The result of all this formidable industrial trade development is a kind of economic break off. South Chinese — something like sixty-five million people — now feel themselves to be financially and psychologically independent of Beijing. And this economic independence now extends to some other provinces. In the face of material progress, ideology and Communist rhetoric are no longer an effective instrument for keeping the remoter provinces under control.

The belief among many Hong Kong Chinese having dealings with the Mainland is that Marxism counts for nothing among ordinary people. "Can you imagine it," said one surprised Hong Kong member of a Mainland family, "there are even unauthorized Christian churches starting up in some of the villages. The Communist cadres still have clout and they still use it to line their pockets, but they drop the Marxist eyewash. It's rather healthy, in a way. They've long since woken up to the fact that it's money that counts. Mind you, this doesn't exactly endear them to the masses but it does introduce a commercial reality into daily life."

Mainland towns and villages are using Hong Kong currency, watching Hong Kong television programmes, listening to Hong Kong popular songs, and generally loosening their roots. In reverse, how are Guangdong's sixty-

five millions going to affect the mere five and three quarter millions in Hong Kong? At present Hong Kong tends to feel complacently superior where its country cousins are concerned, but how long will that persist? When will there come the religious revival, a hunger for simplicity, or a reaction against growth for money's sake? We cannot know what changes are in the air.

Who Speaks the Real Chinese?

Apart from their southern temperament and keen business instincts the Cantonese are distanced from the rest of China by language. Standard national Chinese speech is often called Mandarin because it has always been the official language, though more often it's modified into something called *putonghua* — that is, "common speech" and wherever you go among Chinese people you will find some of them speaking it. Written Chinese is pretty much the same everywhere and it's these written characters or ideograms that have linked all literate Chinese down the centuries, bridging the differing sounds of the local languages and dialects they speak.

However the Cantonese people of Hong Kong have their own spoken dialect. (They even have several hundred of their own ideograms, though these are local and unofficial and you won't find them in the dictionary.) They use racy idioms and proverbs. They absorb foreign words and phrases. But it's a very difficult form of speech, with several more tones or intonations than Mandarin; and Westerners, unless they know they are going to stay out here a long time or intend to become deeply involved with local people, may well be discouraged from learning Cantonese, apart from a few phrases for the market or the taxi driver. It is simply too difficult to retain unless you are going to be conversing in it every day.

Many Cantonese people you meet, however, will hardly admit that anything other than Cantonese is the real Chinese language. In fact they sometimes feel only they are the real Chinese, the people of the ancient Tang dynasty who once occupied much of China before the regrettable barbarians of the North forced them south of the Yangtse.

They will also tell you that certain lines of poetry written during the Tang dynasty — the golden age of Chinese poetic literature — sound and rhyme much better spoken with a Cantonese accent than in Mandarin.

Sometimes, in the villages here in Hong Kong, they find it hard to accept that foreigners can speak the language. The late Ken Barnett, a former Commissioner of Census and fluent Cantonese speaker, once missed his way in the New Territories and asked a couple of old village women for directions. They stared blankly. He repeated his request. No reaction, so he walked on, and as he did so heard one of the women say: "Was that *gweilo* talking Chinese just now? My imagination must be playing tricks."

A curious feature of Cantonese spoken in Hong Kong is the growing use of swearing and foul language. "When I was young," said a university teacher in her fifties," bad language was something used by rougher types — construction workers, labourers, seamen. But for some reason — possibly local films have had an influence — it's spread upwards. A youngish yuppie will drop the odd dirty word, and even girl students talk in a way that would shock their mothers. In a restaurant the language you hear around you at lunch time from middle class office workers can be downright objectionable. But it's spreading — as if people somehow thought it democratic."

Swearing in Cantonese usually refers to turtles' eggs (a very evil connection for some reason) and the status of one's mother. Foreigners picking up Cantonese may think of raising a laugh by using some swear-words. Better not. You are bound to use it in the wrong place with the wrong people.

Not all the Chinese here in Hong Kong are Cantonese though those who come from other provinces soon find it necessary to learn the language if they are going to survive in this Cantonese jungle. Regional dialects are dying out.

You may hear of the Hakkas, a word meaning "guest" or "stranger." These people migrated down here from central and north China. You will see them out in the New Territories, the country districts of Hong Kong, the women wearing those strange hats with black pelmets round the brims. Then there are the boat people who in old days were never allowed to live ashore or take part in examinations and were known as the Tankas ("egg people") a name they find deeply objectionable; and the Hoklo, who are both fishermen and farmers.

At least half a million people living here have their origins in the Shanghai area, at the estuary of the Yangtse. Some of the big local shipping tycoons like the late Sir Y. K. Pao came from Ning Bo, near Shanghai. Shanghai people are the city slickers. When the Communists were taking over the Mainland in 1948 many big Shanghai operators came down to Hong Kong to start new textile and other businesses. They felt they had all it took to boss a provincial business scene like Hong Kong. Some, like Lord Kadoorie and his brother, developed local business empires and were prominent in local philanthropy. Some had lost everything and had to start a new life. "Lots of show-offs," scoffed a southerner, "smart suits and ties but their office address was half a bed space."

If a Shanghai newcomer brought capital he risked being relieved of it and generally taken to the cleaners by the resourceful Cantonese. The tycoon Hardoon was ruined when the stock exchange was rigged against him. Others paid through the nose for house property.

Some of the toughest battles were in the underworld, when Shanghai triads fleeing the Communists tried but failed to take over the Hong Kong dance hall and gambling protection rackets. Those days are long past and intercommunity differences are now somewhat blurred. Shanghai people are by no means all business operators; they merge into the Hong Kong scene in a score of different occupations.

A forceful element on the Hong Kong scene is the Teochew (or Chiuchow) community, who come from the five most easterly counties of Guangdong province. The older generation retain their own dialect and customs and though there is much merging with the local scene, the Teochew identity remains strong. Their part of Guangdong province is mostly poor; when they came to Hong Kong they often did the hardest work, the unloading of cargoes along the Western quays; the dangerous jobs on construction sites. You have to survive somehow. It's been said that the Teochews were the big drug traffickers and the police drug squads were Teochews also.

Some made it to the big time. Enormous prestige has been won for the Teochew community by Li Ka Shing the billionaire developer who has donated a whole university to his home town, Shantou (Swatow) and is known as "superman" in the Hong Kong Chinese press.

The word in Hong Kong is: if you get into a row or dispute, and find out that the people you're quarrelling with are Teochews, then pull out of it quickly. They are bad people to tangle with.

The human map of Hong Kong is changing all the time; different communities intermarry; new ways are pursued and old customs abandoned. Yet strangely enough some societies and organizations based on the past are vigorously surviving. These are local associations whose members all come from the same clan or the same local area on the Mainland. They maintain contact, they help each other, their officers meet regularly.

Hong Kong is going through uncertain times, and when the future is obscure it's best to stick together and remember where your oldest loyalties lie. Even the bar where you meet your friends has a name to remind you of problems ahead. Always, if you're Chinese, you need friends and connections. It reflects the vastness of China with its hundreds of millions of people — a human ocean where the man without life-lines can so easily drown without trace. To a Chinese arriving in Hong Kong it has been an enormous relief to meet, if not a family member, at least someone born in the same village, or a classmate from school or university days. In the 1970s and 1980s these local associations showed signs of losing their relevance; now in the days of run-up to 1997 they seem to offer important hope of neighbourly protection.

As for Western attitudes towards China and the Chinese, their most striking aspect is the sheer ignorance of history and geography they reveal, an ignorance like a distorting cloud obscuring their judgements. The picture of Stanley Baldwin, Prime Minister of the U.K. in the 1930s exclaiming with surprise as he looked at the map with his Foreign Secretary that Shanghai was actually south of Beijing, — this could easily be repeated by the London stockbroker or the engineer come to build a tunnel. How delighted your Chinese acquaintance is when, naming his native province, he hears you pinpoint its geographical position and capital! As for Chinese history, ancient or modern, who in the West, apart from academics, knows anything at all? It is simply not part of British education. Nor have Chinese school students themselves been specially well briefed on the latest chapters of their nation's story. To avoid controversy and possible parental protests and trouble, Chinese history taught in Hong Kong used to come to an end with the death of the Empress Dowager in 1908, though the curriculum has (since 1967) been modernized and expanded.

With the Westerners, and especially with the British new arrivals, ignorance means at least that they don't start with false complexes or guilt feelings. They are probably unaware that there persists, in many Chinese hearts, a resentment at the arrogance and brutality shown by the foreigners — the barbarians — in their behaviour towards the Middle Kingdom. And for decades the British occupied the number one hate position until they moved over to make room for the Japanese. The Japanese are seen to be the worst of all, for Japan's only claim to civilization rests on all the art and philosophy derived from China back in the Tang dynasty — and that then they should have behaved as they did in World War Two ...!

A local Communist official confessed, "The Nixon visit to Beijing was a big enough shock; but that was nothing compared to seeing, on the front page of the *People's Daily*, the picture of Chairman Mao shaking the bloody hand of Tanaka! I couldn't get over that."

When it comes to business today Sino-Japanese exchanges are one of the most dynamic factors in Far East development. Japanese business representatives learn excellent Mandarin and know China better than anyone. The Japanese are the biggest investors in Hong Kong industry, surpassing even the United States. But they haven't been forgiven.

As for Chinese attitudes towards Westerners, especially on the business level, these are much more complex. Hong Kong is different from the Mainland where the Europeans has traditionally been seen as incredibly sophisticated and cunning in business affairs. "Always read the small print with the utmost care," advises a Chinese liaison man. "The British always leave some door open a crack, something hanging. We straightforward Chinese really must look out."

Night signs on Lan Kwai Fong suggest the uncertainty of life after 1997—the urge to congregate in bars and clubs and enjoy life while the going is good.

Ning Po, a city near Shanghai, has seen many of its people make fortunes overseas. Like other migrants arriving in Hong Kong they are glad to make early contact with their residents associations.

I have heard of a patriotic Chinese entrepreneur declaring, twenty years ago, that it was the duty of Chinese to cheat and outsmart the Westerner wherever possible. "It is what they deserve; it is the only way to deal with them."

In Hong Kong that has been replaced by a more tolerant view — that the British, although clumsier and less sensitive than the Chinese, have done a reasonably good job on behalf of Hong Kong business. "They are not so quick on the uptake as us Cantonese," a local businessman will readily admit. "They don't know how to get round corners." However he will agree, without enthusiasm, that the British have fulfilled an important role in keeping pirates away, establishing some law and order, and then leaving it to the Chinese to get on with creating the wealth and the jobs.

What emerges from all this is the difficulty of summing up Chinese feelings towards Westerners in a single phrase. Everything depends on the particular circumstances and kind of contact. Chinese people take Westerners as they find them, though if things go sour then of course that is a sign of barbarism and lack of understanding of Chinese civilization, and in no time at all we are brooding on the Opium Wars.

So many influences are at work. A Chinese may be more survival-conscious than a Westerner, more keenly aware of the disaster that threatens when least expected. But whether your morality is based on Confucius, or on Christianity (there are half a million Christians in Hong Kong), or Buddhism, everyone has a fair idea of decency and villany. The Chinese may be men and women of the great world; or sometimes their mental isolation comes as a shock. For every dozen families who know nothing of the West you will find another keenly interested in Europe or the States, who's long enjoyed warm and profitable relationships with Westerners, their children have gone to school and university in Britain; human links are strong. Their next door neighbours, who may have had an unpleasant taste of arrogance and superi-ority on the part of their colonial masters, will harbour very different feelings. No two cases are the same.

In Hong Kong you may also come across Chinese who, apart from their appearance and ancestry, are scarcely Chinese at all. Their forefathers went abroad many generations ago in search of fortune; and they themselves have been educated in foreign-speaking schools and lack any knowledge of Chinese language. They speak a broad Australian or English; when they visit Hong Kong in search of their roots their linguistic shortcomings may give them an embarrassing time in shops and restaurants. And they, too, may have to take advice on Chinese etiquette and rules of behaviour as fast as they can, if they're not to suffer rebuke and even insult.

So this is the scene confronting the newcomer. A challenging scene, you may say; but enlivened by rewards and unexpected compensations. In some ways Chinese seem no different from the rest of the world; one is impressed by their down-to-earth commonsense and logic. But they are not like the rest and the ways in which they differ, the way they follow instincts, traditions and superstitions unsuspected by the Westerner — that is the special factor, the puzzle of knowing and living alongside the Chinese.

Chapter 5

Birthday Celebrations — Or?

For Chinese married couples the birth of a son has always been the happiest of events, calling for joyful congratulations all round.

"Isn't that the same everywhere in the world?" asks your Chinese friend.

Well, not to the same extent. Chinese set such store by the survival of the family, continuance of the name, the assurance after death of a kind of immortality because of the respectful rites observed by generations of descendants.

What about girls? They are less important, says the traditionalist. You see, they will get married in due course, become part of somebody else's family and so lost to you. It's the sons who preserve the name — as well as taking care of the parents in their old age.

A Chinese man is delighted when he becomes grandfather to a healthy boy and knows the family line is assured for another generation.

Needless to say such ideas have been subjected to steady erosion in Hong Kong with the passing years.

You can still find many families consisting of four or five daughters followed by youngest child, a son. Mother has gone on trying until she fulfils her destiny. But nowadays girls are much more acceptable in Hong Kong than before. A wife's failure to produce a boy is no longer grounds for divorce or the excuse to take a second spouse. Whatever your sex, when you arrive on a Hong Kong family scene you can be pretty sure of a warm and loving welcome. And of course nowadays it's possible to know beforehand how things are going to turn out. Congratulate a mother-to-be on her lovely looks which indicate, according to the old wives' tale that it's going to be a boy and she may well reply: "Well, actually we've had the tests; we know what it's going to be already." Anyway, hearty congratulations are in order.

Everyone in Hong Kong knows things are different on the Mainland. There giving birth may be a criminal act. One child per family is the rule and if you have more than one you may find yourself in deep trouble.

In Hong Kong the birthrate has dropped steeply but without any regulation by Government. Family planning is widely practised. Some couples postpone parenthood because of uncertainties after 1997. Some feel that with two or three children instead of five or six the whole family stands a better chance in the world; and you will meet young professional couples who want to enjoy life first before thinking about babies. Ideas about safeguarding the health of mother and child have changed over the years in Hong Kong, largely due to advances in medical science. Mothers attend antenatal clinics and have their deliveries in hospitals or maternity homes. Lately a controversy arose over some mothers preferring to call doctors instead of qualified and experienced midwives. It was suggested that doctors tend to focus on aided delivery when that might not be really necessary. One doctor said that many heavier babies are being born by young Chinese mothers these days because of more nourishing diets; in a growing number of cases their narrow pelvises are too slight to cope; and that this partly explains the increasing number of Caesarean births.

But the level of perinatal mortality in Hong Kong is well below that recorded in the West. In fact it is one of the lowest in the world.

Chinese mothers do what the clinic tells them. They also listen to the lessons of four thousand years. Even sophisticated professional women will go along with customs passed on by grandparents.

Sometimes strange taboos are observed. No melons or bananas (and certainly no snakes!) to be eaten during the months of pregnancy. Otherwise

the child may be born with defective organs or suffer from eczema.

"The great thing is peace and quite," said a Chinese mother. "Everything must stay the same, the bed mustn't be moved, no interior decoration undertaken, no banging of hammers, no knocking in nails." It's thought advisable by many (you find this also in the West) to surround the expectant mother with beautiful objects, to induce calm and positive emotions. These will result in beautiful children.

There's a deep faith in the tonic effects of ginger. One of the complaints of immigrants from the Mainland in the famine years of the early sixties was the lack of ginger for nursing mothers.

The wife of a high-level Chinese Hong Kong official who had just given birth, explained to a Western friend why she couldn't be visited for the month ahead. It seems her mother-in-law is one of the old-fashioned kind and as soon as the mother and baby could leave hospital they went straight round to a bedroom at mother-in-law's place to stay there for a month under a special regime. She would take almost no exercise, never have a bath but be washed only in specially boiled water, never wash her hair, and generally keep well covered up and protected.

The strictly-controlled diet included, needless to say, large quantities of ginger. And all that month the husband was not allowed to put a foot inside the room.

Some ancient cultures consider women become unclean in giving birth, and that therefore they must be kept segregated for a set period in order to avoid contaminating other household members. But for Chinese the main objective of the seclusion has been to protect the health of the mother for the sake of future offspring. And the best way of doing that, according to the older generation of Chinese mothers-in-law, is to keep her snug in bed. Exercise? Forget it.

Even modern thinking Chinese women feel there may be something in this purdah exercise. It has often been said that Chinese mothers who take these precautions are less likely to suffer from rheumatism and arthritis in later life. And anyway, what people have been doing for thousands of years must have some deep, traditional sense behind it.

It is often said that Chinese parents love their children and show their love more than Westerners do. In a holiday crowd you are far less likely to hear whimpering or crying among Chinese children than in the West; they are always being picked up and patted and included in the conversation and their first tottering steps taken to choruses of enthusiastic applause.

However it sometimes seems that loving attention starts when the child has developed a personality, and not from the days when it's still not much more than a demanding consumer unable to speak or act reasonably.

You will meet a working professional couple in Hong Kong who, not long after the baby is weaned, are farming it out to a professional minder, collecting it only at weekends. And often then, if they are busy with work or other commitments, they will phone the minder to tell her they won't be calling round to collect until the following week. The parents seemed to think it no great matter, though it would shock Western psychologists with their theories of the importance of "bonding" in early childhood.

Sometimes it's a matter of both parents having to work to keep the family going or to save for the future. Hong Kong life is largely based on husband and wife both earning.

Nothing in Hong Kong life more betrays the variety of thinking and tradition here than the way people celebrate — or ignore — the birthday anniversary. In the Chinese family tradition, especially among the old-fashioned and lower-wage-earners children's birthdays hardly count. No birthday cakes or parties or presents. Many Chinese people in Hong Kong would not be able to tell you their exact date of birth, unless it was noted for some official purpose. (Though some parents conscientious about horoscopes will note not only the date but the time of day.)

"It all depends where your family comes from," said a housing-estate daughter. "I come from the boat people and I remember that when I was young my mother would cook a meal with eggs on my birthday. My school friend's mother used to take her out with the rest of the family for a nice chicken meal in the neighbourhood restaurant. But no presents and no birthday cards. I remember sending my mother a card for her birthday and she was downright embarrassed. She knew she shouldn't just throw it away but there seemed to be no place for it."

The birthdays celebrated in some families are the landmarks — for instance when a man attains the important age of twenty which means he is mature; or sixty, representing the dignity of old age. And every birthday after sixty will be celebrated, showing the respect due to longevity and experience.

Another strongly entrenched belief assigns particular importance to the ages of forty-nine, fifty-nine and so on. If a man reaches the ninth year of his decade, so to speak, he will certainly last until the next ninth year. So if a man seriously ill nevertheless manages to make it to his forty-ninth or fifth-ninth birthday then he is certainly good for another ten years. The fact that this often doesn't happen seems to leave the belief undisturbed.

Some Hong Kong people are convinced that a birthday must always be celebrated on or before the date and that to do so afterwards brings bad luck. Others dismiss this as rubbish.

Sometimes it's only while working abroad that the young Hong Konger comes to know birthday pleasures. A Hong Kong Chinese student recalls his time at a British university when he shared rooms in a hostel with half a dozen others, most of them British but including a German girl. "And the Germans are really crazy when it comes to anniversaries. We all had to tell our birthdays (I made mine up) and every birthday we had a party, with a cake, and toasts and a good time generally. And if your birthday fell in vacation time this German girl would fix a substitute date for later. It's one of my happiest student memories."

Year after year Hong Kong changes under the influence of the world outside. Children's birthday parties are much more common though not in every family. The young son at the government school attended by children of boat people and taxi drivers wanted to know why his sister (Form Five at St. Stephen's) was always being invited to birthday parties and he never was.

The China Mainland shows a very different scene. This is the second largest country in the world with one of the smallest relative areas of farmland, and the apparently unstoppable growth of the population is a national nightmare.

Most Mainland Chinese are farmers and you can't convince a farmer that sons aren't useful at planting and harvest time. And if you point out that, in the south at least, girls work in the fields, they will say you must have a son to carry on the family name. Unremitting efforts by the authorities to enforce the one-child family meet with success in the much supervised cities. But out in the countryside it's a different story. Old prejudices against girls survive there; and the problem (in both city and provinces) is aggravated by shifting armies of casual workers who slip through the control net and produce millions of unregistered infants.

In such a vast child-loving country stories abound of hardship, bribery of officials, street committees keeping a hawk-like eye on local pregnancies, and of female children simply abandoned or killed so that the one surviving child shall be a boy. In one case a woman gave birth to a child which died the following day. Then she learned that after having had the one child she had been sterilized in the hospital without her knowledge, so she could not have any more — a wretched fate for a Chinese woman.

If there's one aspect of the Mainland regime which turns Hong Kong people off, it's the enforced family planning and abortions.

Yet what are the authorities to do? They were hoping to keep the country's population below a thousand million up to the year two thousand. Only thus would their advances in industry and farming raise living standards. Now they are 200 million over the top and every extra million is an obstacle to progress.

So the one-child family, already enforced in the cities, is being followed up in the countryside and even in the areas of the minority peoples, the Miaos, the Yis, the Chuangs, who were formerly free of restriction. Nobody in China likes the idea of one child. Everyone knows the disadvantages. Stories abound of little monsters now growing up in urban families, centres of attention and affection by parents and grandparents, and thoroughly spoiled. These single children, it is said, are becoming overweight and a phenomenon quite new for China has appeared — classes for weight-reduction. Then there is the teeth problem. Single male children are given so many sweets that their teeth suffer and nowadays dentists thrive. Waiting lists are very long; it may cost you a bottle of liquor or theatre tickets just to be sure of an appointment.

Chapter 6

Chinese Women

Chinese women are different from the rest. Mostly they are more intelligent than Chinese men, (university honours graduates are nearly all girls) though they tend to play this down. Their variety is infinite.

You can meet a softly-spoken lady of enormous dignity who seems to have stepped straight out of a Tang dynasty poem. Her daughter, just returned on vacation from an American university, expresses her personality in a very different way; yet the mother's influence is discernible. Over all Chinese womanhood hangs a cloud of conservatism. For most of them marriage and the care of children is the only acceptable fate (although in Hong Kong a clever and strong-willed girl can resist the pressure).

They are more natural and direct in manner than women from the West. When they are beautiful they

Variety of Chinese women. Buxom farmers' daughters become child amahs, join an ancient family.

seem not to parade it and this can be disconcerting as well as disarming. The conversation of film actresses and beauty competition winners is down-to-earth and sometimes penetrating, as if it were accepted that a thick head, however pretty, is a grave drawback to survival in the tough Hong Kong arena. Filial piety takes a practical form. Ask a film star what she is going to do with all that money and she tells you about the plan to buy a flat for her mother. Behind every film star there's a mother, acting as a guardian agent.

You have to be bright, and know how to dress. Young women executives and office secretaries love brand name couture, which is big business in Hong Kong, and the less well-off do very well on export rejects. It's a Westernized scene, in sharp contrast to that of even twenty years ago when the Chinese cheongsam — high collar and slit skirt, elegant on the figure but a trial in the summer heat — was the universal uniform.

The story of Chinese womanhood — in Hong Kong and elsewhere — is contradictory and sometimes tragic; and newcomers to the Far East may not be aware of it, because they are unfamiliar with China's past. It's a story of power, self-sacrifice and ruthless exploitation. Traditional characters are the docile wife who keeps silent when her husband is out carousing with companions or making love with his concubines; and the unacknowledged saint, protectress of small children. A different persona — though it has been known to coexist in the same physical frame — is that of the matriarch running the extended family, restraining the intrigues of secondary wives and mistresses. But that largely belongs to a grandmotherly past and literary tradition. It's twenty years now since it was legal for a man in Hong Kong to have as many wives as he could afford. We are in a time of transition.

Today's family households here (and in most Mainland areas) are small and nuclear and certainly in Hong Kong women have been achieving greater freedom and there's a continuing steady pressure for greater equality as well.

The whole status of women has come under vigorous scrutiny. Night after night television programmes in Hong Kong (in between the scenes of violence) unintentionally stress the contrast between the way women live in the Western world and in British colonialist Hong Kong. The Hong Kong woman is so often less assertive, more reluctant to start a good healthy row to clear the air.

Of course there are exceptions but until recently, at least on the China Mainland, women could rarely expect anything but conditions of inferiority and bleak injustice, institutionalized and taken for granted. You may say there's been discrimination against women in the West too, but it's nothing compared with what Chinese women have had to endure. Even now a Chinese woman can't take considerate treatment for granted.

Newcomers may be surprised when they realize that among the Chinese there is no tradition of gallantry or chivalry of making way for women, opening doors, giving up a seat. They are not regarded as the weaker sex. (Chivalry's dying out in the West, too, to the applause of some.) Strangely enough, some Western customs of masculine politeness are being encouraged these days by the younger Hong Kong generation. If a group is out on a walking expedition, the girls will tease a young man if he doesn't volunteer to ask the way or organize the transport home. This is a recent phenomenon.

Sexual harassment? That's a likely hazard of daily life but still less of a curse than the rules of Confucius. He insisted on women's submissiveness. They must be obedient to mothers-in-law, husband and sons. To a surprising

extent Confucius has survived most attempts to change things. Old attitudes are condemned in theory but the Chinese world is still run by men for men. Mainland bureaucracy protects the macho evil doer. Your wife is harassed and raped by a powerful official; make too much fuss about it and you may well end in jail. This actually happened to someone I know.

Both on the Mainland and in Hong Kong many women work, usually to help meet family expenses. Hong Kong women are divided far more sharply by income than by temperament. The world of the working poor here is light-years away from the comfort and ostentation of the business achievers; yet even very rich women in Hong Kong would usually reject a butterfly existence. The warm-hearted and socially aware among them work for the underprivileged; the business-minded go in for acquisitive projects. A hard-headed tycoon husband may be ready to finance a do-good plan in return for some favour from officialdom and it's his wife who will be sitting on the committee — giving up part of her leisure to organize help for the old, sick and helpless — as well as running her own business.

The rich do include the overindulged human ornament, waking in the morning to reach for the phone to arrange the next mah-jong party, spending on clothes and jewellery in a month as much as a building worker earns in two years. But idleness is very alien to Hong Kong, which is a place of active, positive people — including women — where the very air breathes opportunity.

Professional women abound here — talented women journalists, business-women, lawyers, academics, administrators, charity organizers, senior police officers. Bilingual women secretaries command high salaries.

In public life there is a special type of woman — colloquially known as a *nüqiangren* — a "strong lady" who figures largely in the news of the territory. The term is at once admiring and jokingly critical. Such women are very much a symbol of Hong Kong, of its vitality, commonsense, ability to control people and situations.... Usually they come from well-off families and inherit the tough qualities of their parents or grandparents. Sometimes they have been educated at prestige Western girls' schools and universities. This is obviously a great asset when they return to Hong Kong and enter business or politics. It

At the Tai Hung Cotton Mill on Castle Peak Road, one girl looks after eight hundred spindles.

means that in contact with British directors or colonial officials they express themselves — in English — intelligently and with force. Not surprisingly, women of this background have often been chosen by the colonial authorities for influential positions.

They are very much a part of today's world and far less influenced than their mothers by Chinese traditional culture. "Their Chinese calligraphy is quite appalling," complained an elderly professor. "I saw some of them write their names in the welcome book at a great wedding. It was as if they were using an axe instead of a brush."

"People joke about 'strong women'," complained a local feminist. "But they simply take 'strong men' as normal. That shows how unfairly women are discriminated against."

Many professional women seem to keep family and husbands well in the background. They marry a man they've known since childhood, have children, and continue their careers with minimal interruption.

Yet Hong Kong also abounds in conscientious mothers. An impressive personality here is that of the Chinese married woman in her middle thirties with three young children of school age, devoting her time to worrying about their health, happiness, manners and progress at school. In no place in the world will you come across so many mothers supervising their children's homework. They seem to care less about themselves. Either that or they find most fulfilment in helping their children get a head start.

As in other parts of the world, family life is women's creation. If under pressure of debts, husband's neglect and multiple worries she finally gives up the struggle, then the whole domestic structure collapses. Social workers will tell you there's no hell so terrifying as the small overcrowded flat dominated by a neurotic and unbalanced wife. Heaven only knows the abuse cases unrecorded, children growing up in a private scene of nightmares and menace.

Yet it's well to remember how life in Hong Kong has improved for many, through public opinion, pressures of religious bodies and legislation. The full study of Chinese womanhood on the Mainland has still to be written. How heroic seem the reforms introduced by Chairman Mao when he took power in China in 1949. And few now recall that, long before the Communists came, women's groups were already fighting to secure education and a measure of freedom, a parallel to the history of womanhood in the Western world but with harsh Confucian additions and emphasis. Their efforts make the struggle for Western women's suffrage look like a Sunday picnic.

By sheer persistence they gained entry to local middle schools and endured the pain of unbinding their feet in order to join in physical exercises in the school gymnasium, to the jeering of onlookers. Some acquired enough education to become teachers; the formerly illiterate mother of Ding Ling,

From a balcony in Central the future for a secretary or woman manager looks ten times as bright as ten years ago, but opportunities are still restricted.

Business leader Miss Patsy Chang, one of Hong Kong's new wave of "strong ladies". She is a director of the Po Leung Kok, a leading charitable organization.

the woman writer, became a headmistress.

In Hong Kong the colonial government, sometimes under pressure from London or local women's groups, has abolished a man's right to have official secondary wives or concubines. It has also outlawed a system whereby young girls were sold into families needing domestic servants. Chinese wives no longer have to tolerate married life shared with a newcomer intriguing for the husband's favours. They have the right to divorce. A widow can marry again, as long as she is discreet about it and the relatives don't make too much fuss.

And talking of reforms it's good to remember that already eighty years ago the Chinese were abandoning the custom of foot-binding. "Yes, I agree," says your Chinese colleague, "a most unhealthy custom — just as bad as the tight-lacing your Victorian ladies inflicted on themselves, also with the aim of attracting a prospective husband." It might be replied, to keep the argument going, that tight-lacing was the personal decision of an adult, not a torture inflicted on a child. The influence of foot-binding on female psychology and, indirectly, on family and social life in a crucial era is a huge and repulsive subject still to be researched.

"Is it really true," asked a Chinese teacher, "that in your Christian marriage ceremony bride and bridegroom agree to take each other 'for richer, for poorer, in sickness and health' and, most important, 'forsaking all other.'?" That is very different from our Chinese attitude. We do not expect the husband to forsake his parents. In fact he continues to observe great obligations towards them, more than towards his wife."

Until recently a woman was a chattel. In the countryside, she did not even have a name of her own; she was simply "Sister" prefixed by a number, or "So-and-so's wife."

Even today, in the countryside area of Hong Kong's New Territories, women in some villages are not allowed to enter ancestral halls. A male villager has the right to build himself a house, but women cannot. Nor do they inherit family savings.

"We sign a paper renouncing claims to family inheritance," says a daughter in the village.

"You mean you sign under duress?"

"No, we just sign. We always do this."

The dead hopelessness of ancient days. Yet their children may go off to work and study in the modern world of the city, travel abroad for holidays, win distinction at universities in faraway lands, enjoy all the freedoms.

The Hong Kong Council of Women has protested that although most women in Hong Kong earn wages from jobs besides running the home, they are paid less than men doing the same work, and when they do piecework at home they are not protected by labour laws and get no written contracts.

"If your wife and your father were drowning, whom would you first hasten to save?" is a question less easily answered nowadays than fifty years ago. That shows something about the improving status of women although,

Kai-yin Lo designs jewellery and is known worldwide.

needless to say, wives with strong personalities or special qualities have come to dominate the marriage, even in the darkest days of male tyranny. The cheering message of modern times is the range of professional opportunities open to girls. Even a lady of modest and retiring temperament will admit that she has been called to the bar, or has a degree in business management.

A brilliant, lively Hong Kong girl bemoaned her failure to get a university place despite having passed the entrance examinations, but still insisted Hong Kong was a good place for a professional woman. "I have the feeling that here I can do just about anything I want — study computers, earn a good salary as a manageress, start my own business. Of course you have to work, learn English, keep on with studies. But no one sets out to stop you doing what you want. And when you've saved some money you can travel and see something of the world."

Chinese women generally do more than men to look after and care for aged parents — like the heroine in a Mainland TV series. They are expected to be self-sacrificing as a matter of course. A woman married to a notoriously unfaithful husband is not expected to leave him. Rather she will acquire face among her friends because she puts up with his evil ways without making a fuss about it. And if economic crisis strikes the family she is expected to play an equal role with the husband in meeting it, taking the strain alone if he falls out.

But she is not, however humble the home, expected to descend to begging. That is against all received ideas of Chinese etiquette and custom. There are few beggars in the streets of Hong Kong and the women among them are nearly old, gnarled creatures — grandmothers sent to the tourist-frequented areas by their mercenary children to swell the family income.

The half-crazed and very abject, hiding in corners, mentally handicapped or unhinged victims of too extreme unkindness or ingratitude — they usually refuse money. They have rejected the world, opted out. An exception was a confused girl in a terribly neglected state but found to be carrying several hundred dollars, nearly all in filthy ten cent coins which had to be counted at the police station. The enthusiastic new woman inspector who'd arrested her was very unpopular that month and afterwards left ragged derelicts alone.

Sometimes women beg for a special reason. The creature lurking along Des Voeux Road near the Gloucester Building (now the Landmark) in the early 1960s — she fitted no known category. Who could she be?

Her hair was caught up at the sides in ringlets, a style quite strange to Hong Kong; and then her approach was unusual. She did not actually beg with her hand out but rather moved quietly alongside her target. The expression of pleading and despair — it was unnatural, embarrassing. Then, as soon as you held out some coins she grabbed them as if afraid they might be withdrawn, and vanished in the crowd.

It turned out that she was the wife of a former Nationalist Army general and they were living with their two young sons out at Rennie's Mill, a squatter area where many of the retreating Chiang Kai-shek troops and their families had taken refuge after the 1949 Mainland take-over. The general had been the associate of an army commander who'd fallen out of favour, which explained why he had not gone to Taiwan with his colleagues. He was too ill to work now and the family lived in a hut and survived in a hand-to-mouth way, on some kind of army pension and occasional sums from charitable organizations.

The wife begged for a special, separate reason — to put enough money aside (with extra cash from one or two philanthropic societies) to send both the sons to university. For years she begged, out in all weathers. When last heard of one of the sons was already in college and his brother was expected soon to follow him.

Even more determined was seventeen-year-old Mei-ling, stay and support of five brothers and sisters but taken to hospital with tuberculosis. Mother dead years ago, father a TB out-patient. Mei-ling, small and insignificant if you met her in the street, is very clever, always top of her class and the hope had been that she'd enter university, get a teaching job, bring the whole family up out of the depths. So when she caught TB it was a terrible blow. You might think it would be the end — father drifting into drugs, children wandering the streets.

But not at all. Mei-ling had worked it out and reckoned that, if the hospital could get her patched up by the time spring term started in January, she could catch up well enough to pass the summer exam that would get her into university with her fees paid. She managed a good deal of studying in the hospital ward. After she was discharged she'd still have to attend a TB clinic for many months before being finally cured, but when last heard of she was starting university with every hope of landing a good job later. This would take care of things until her small brothers and sisters were educated and launched in the world.

Stories like this are common enough in Hong Kong, where there's not much time to be young and reckless. You're needed very early on, if you're bright and your parents are hard up. The interesting aspect, from the outsider's point of view, was that no one in her family seemed to think

Mothers in Hong Kong bring up children on small budgets, see them to kindergarten and school, and worry over their homework.

Mei-ling's effort at all unusual. It was what you would expect from a Hong Kong Chinese girl. It's the lives and work of the anonymous thousands — the united, hardworking families — that keep the Hong Kong machine revolving smoothly and at high speed. In their unsensational world old-fashioned morality and rules of conduct are taken for granted. Yet perhaps this is changing, like so much else. Does the Chinese girl contemplating marriage look for new qualities in a future husband, expect a different kind of life from that endured by her mother?

In Hong Kong the meek, long-suffering heroine is no longer the great model. Stranger still, it's not only gone out of fashion on the Mainland but there's growing debate on the romantic aspects of marriage and the dreary wastefulness of unions without love and affection. All a result, the analysts say, of the changes that came in the late 1970s and brought easier material conditions to many households, more time for women to think about their lives. But more of that later.

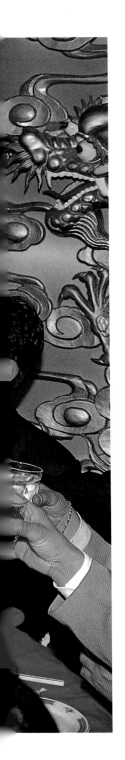

Chapter 7

Weddings
— And After

Marriage is a great Chinese institution and the Westerner had better be prepared. Sooner or later he or she will be invited to a Chinese wedding and it's as well to ask for advice on what is expected of the guest.

The registry office part is brief enough (all weddings in Hong Kong have to be registered now). There's no more pleasing sight on a sunny day than the young bridal pairs being photographed on the steps of the garden outside the City Hall office. Almost certainly the whole bride's outfit has been hired, even including the false eye-lashes, but it's been chosen with enormous care, and the effect is one of nervous radiance and charm. The Westerner will probably be invited not to the registry office but to the reception at a restaurant which follows early in the evening. For this he must study the invitation, hand-

The wedding feast crowns the day of rites and ceremonies. The whole floor of a restaurant is rented with a hundred tables or more, and many toasts are drunk.

somely printed in scarlet and gold, and all in Chinese characters needing translation.

The bridegroom may be the cheerful office boy one has come to know and like over the months, and the bride the little girl who brings in the mail. Do not expect, because of this, that the reception will be a modest, quiet affair in some back room. Arriving at the restaurant you will soon find that a whole floor has been taken over. You sign your name with a Chinese brush and are led into a great assemblage of fifty tables full of people, all finishing their mah-jong games before the feast begins.

The bride and bridegroom greet you as if you are their most valued friends. The bride is dazzling. She has changed her dress and instead of something from the bridal pages of Vogue now suggests something dynastic from Peking opera — a gown of stiff scarlet flowered brocade, with a bouquet of flowers. She will probably change again during the evening, for the moment when she and her new husband kneel to offer tea ceremonially to the parents.

You may be the only non-Chinese presence in this crowded, animated room. They seem to go to extraordinary lengths to make you feel at home. At your table the young people who look after you are all English-speaking as if chosen for that purpose. They seem to take it for granted that you'll be drinking brandy by the tumblerful. You are photographed with the bride and bride-groom, with their parents, with their friends. This is a symbolic announcement by determined people that their coming together shall be known to the whole world, even to the most distant parts of the non-Chinese universe.

I have never been able to check on this satisfactorily but I have a suspicion that, for Chinese, the introduction of a completely non-Chinese element, in strict moderation, means something positive, may even bring luck. Many years ago, exploring the more thoroughly Chinese part of Hong Kong, my wife and I strayed into a restaurant and suddenly found ourselves confronted by a dazzling group that included a beaming young girl and dignified older people. And although we excused ourselves for gate-crashing a private affair they seemed to do their very best to persuade us to stay. It must have been a Chinese wedding though we were too new and ignorant in those days to realize what was afoot.

When the bridegroom and his friends call for the bride on the wedding morning, tradition obliges him to provide money in red envelopes for the bridesmaids. There's bargaining and teasing before they settle on the sum.

A wedding present? Of course you have brought a reasonable amount of cash in a red envelope. All the guests have done the same. Otherwise how could the office messenger possibly face the cost of this unforgettable day?

As for the individual amount, this is settled by telephoning among the guests beforehand. Sometimes the bride's office friends will club together to buy some welcome gift — say, a TV set. In that case they won't be expected to contribute to the cost of the wedding reception.

With the rich, things are different. As for the very rich, your eyes dazzle. A multi-multi-millionaire may load his daughter with diamonds and precious metals, with the dresses such as to arouse deep emotion in the heart of a top *couturière*. It's father's way of showing the world what a great man he is.

Ordinary couples take a more pragmatic view. A girl clerk said she and her boyfriend would be taking no holidays this year; they'd be getting married. How much would that cost? She mentioned a figure — seventy thousand Hong Kong dollars — that seemed appalling. "Well, just look at it," she said.

"You've got the down payment on the flat and the legal expenses; you've got the wedding, with the restaurant charging something like two thousand dollars a table at least, and then the brandy and wine; and then you know, in the new place, everything has to be completely new, right down to the last mat and handkerchief." Though the programme varies according to community and family background and parental influence, a wedding is a big event, with no false economy.

Whatever you do, don't give a clock as a present. The Cantonese word for clock sounds the same as the word meaning "end" or "finish".

Not so very long ago marriage among Chinese people was an inordinately complicated and prolonged business transaction, a deal between two families each expecting to gain in strength and dignity through the contract. And still today, in parts of the New Territories and among the boat people ancient customs are followed. The bride may still be taken to her new home in a red-covered sedan chair or by boat; there are elaborate rules of exchanging presents, including a roast pig when the marriage has been duly and satisfac-torily consummated. One kind of wedding ceremony you almost certainly will

The bride is conducted from her parents' home under a red umbrella. Red is the auspicious colour.

not be invited to attend is a marriage of ghosts. They are still held in Hong Kong, though very rarely. Sometimes one of the bridal pair is dead, sometimes both. The living groom who marries a deceased wife is said to have "taken to himself a ghost wife", while the bride who marries a deceased man "marries by embracing the tablet of the deceased". When both groom and bride are dead their parents will hire a go-between to draw up the contract between the two families.

Ceremonies for posthumous weddings used to be just as elaborate as those for the living. The main difference was that at the ghost weddings paper presents would be burned, so that the couple would have the use of them in the next world. Relatives and friends would escort the bride's coffin to the groom's burial ground, and the coffin was laid beside that of the husband; and from this time on the dead couple were considered to be locked in a husband-wife relationship.

How has the custom of ghost marriages come about? Sometimes two families have wanted to form an alliance but the prospective bride or bridegroom died unexpectedly. And sometimes, it has been said, a certain visitant has appeared in a dream and later been identified as a once living eligible bride or bridegroom.

All this belongs to an era when marriage represented very much a contractual deal between families and the feelings of the young people concerned were unimportant. A bridegroom might not see his bride before the wedding day. Nowadays in Hong Kong Western films and education have revolutionized attitudes.

There is still pressure on young women to get married. Families need successors, descendants, though even here Hong Kong is influenced by outside factors, films, books, television. A vigorous, highly intelligent secretary in her late twenties says: "I'll marry when the right man comes along. And by that I mean the man who's right for me. Not just anyone."

Bad luck being a girl, a Westerner said; you couldn't just go up to a man and suggest marriage. The girl secretary laughed. "Can't you? You'd be surprised, today in Hong Kong."

Thirty years ago a girl would consider it a very serious matter to become engaged to a man her parents disapproved of. "That's not true any more," said a young salesgirl. "Nowadays we look for the man we'll decide will be right for us; we don't marry to please parents." That attitude is not universal. In more conservative families parental voices are listened to very respectfully. However these days far fewer families consult a matchmaker.

Wedding invitations are works of printers' art—gold on a red background.

Often in the past a young Mainlander, married to a village girl and the father of her children, has come alone to Hong Kong in search of a steady job, with the aim of bringing the family along later. Life here has bristled with problems, at least in the early stages; he has found it difficult to save money or find a comfortable place to live. His wife cannot get an exit visa. Years pass and he finds a new wife in Hong Kong, and they start a new family.

"He sends money back to his first wife and she and the new wife accept the situation," says a social worker. "Often those queues at the border at Lunar New Year include many grown-ups and children returning to visit the husband's first family."

"I can't exactly remember when we were told that we had these stepbrothers and stepsisters back in Guangdong," says a young teacher, "but my real mother never seemed to make a fuss about it. We see our Mainland relatives about twice a year and we all get on all right."

Marriage situations of this kind are not always so trouble-free. Often it's a case of a Mainlander leaving his wife and children behind and then abandoning them completely when he finds a girlfriend in Hong Kong. This happens in dozens of cases. And it's difficult, given the lack of lawyers and conventional legal aid in Mainland China, for the neglected wife to get a fair deal.

The result of all the uncertainty and restlessness of Hong Kong life is that young women tend to be more cautious in courtship and marriage.

"In the West," said the Chinese wife, "I know of marriages that started with love affairs on holiday and everything was romantic and rosy-coloured; and they hardly knew each other. In Hong Kong girls tend to be more careful and down-to-earth. You have to love him, but you want to know what he's earning and the sort of woman his mother is."

Year by year, here in Hong Kong, an erratic process of change causes the breaking-down of social rules thought until now to be unchallengeable. What is daring and avant-garde to one age-group is so acceptable to its successors as to be hardly worth the bother of discussing. Sleep with your boyfriend? Well, you expect marriage if a baby's on the way. But that's not always the satisfactory answer. The modern Chinese personality casts aside the rules of ancestors but after a time of freedom finds the new environment cold and dark and again looks for support in customs and usages taught in childhood. The vigorous young men and women in their twenties and thirties find themselves quite out of tune with the next generation, the restless teenagers. Sometimes you will feel in Hong Kong there are as many points of view on the basics of life as there are families.

Mixed marriages, once very rare, are now far more common. Are they a success? Impossible to generalize for every one is different. A marriage has most chance of success when a Chinese girl marries a Westerner rather than the other way found. As with most marriages everywhere, the higher the intelligence of both partners the better the chances. They will always have something to talk about.

A Chinese woman intellectual now living in Britain said: "If and when a Chinese and a Westerner marry they must have respect for each other's way of life and habits and tolerate the shortcomings of the other's culture. Westerners tend to be cold towards the other's relatives, friends and acquaintance, and they show it. Chinese may not understand enough the importance the West attaches to privacy; and Chinese women may be more guilty of fussing or nagging out of worry for their husbands, while Western men tend to be less caring because they don't want to interfere in the wife's privacy. There is no such thing as privacy in most Chinese families though of course there can always be secrets!"

A visiting psychologist said mixed marriages run into trouble when the Chinese husband, having married a European somewhere abroad, is anxious to prove to his conservative parents on his return that he is a perfectly good and filial son despite this lapse. This is often more than the Western wife can stand.

In one unusual marriage the American wife chose a Chinese answer. Her conservative father-in-law had made his second son warn the erring older boy that terrible things would happen if he married the gweilo; but this meant that when the sinner persisted in his folly the father, having threatened only indirectly, could now smile and accept without losing face. In fact the new husband was given the same allowance as the other sons. And the foreign wife, already fluent in Chinese, took it upon herself to study the family archives, meet all the relatives and acquire an extensive knowledge of family protocol and festival celebrations. To this end she asked the advice of the family women members, thus assuming a commendably inferior position. The children of this highly successful marriage were brought up as Chinese.

Closer to the tough world of today's Hong Kong is the story of the hardworking German garage manager married to the handsome, lacquered Shanghai woman who spent all his money and robbed him of his self-respect, until he threw up his well-paid job and returned penniless to Stuttgart to escape from her.

For many years young men from Hong Kong's New Territories have gone to European cities to work in the Chinese restaurants there. Some have married European girls. "But these are not true marriages," said a village elder. "We do not recognize these women; they are dead to us." Although the Hong Kong world is changing so fast, the deep-rooted conservatism of village life persists like a coral reef just below the surface. When the Chinese farmer marries the European girl he's unlikely to bring her back to his village.

Yet there have been times when the Britishness of Hong Kong, the solidity and strength of British capitalism and independent system of justice have been a beacon light for Chinese looking for security and survival. When the Chinese Nationalist regime was finally collapsing, the Communists were moving in, and all was chaos and uncertainty, the Western world seemed to offer the only life-raft for many. Some middle class Chinese girls were being urged by their parents to find Western husbands. An elderly acquaintance once said: "I was a young and romantic landlord's son in Beijing, I heard my girlfriend and her family were having a hard time after moving down to Hong Kong; so I followed them to see what I could do. I offered her marriage but she said she didn't need me; her plan was to marry a rich American." And another man, a Chinese intellectual, was told by the university teacher he had his eyes on that she was looking for a Western marriage but if nothing worked out, then she might possibly consider him.

This is no general commentary on female psychology, simply a reflection of dangerous and uncertain times, which never seem far round the corner if you're born Chinese.

With the great handover of 1997 looming closer the asylum offered by the West becomes more important than ever. Some Hong Kong marriages are breaking up through the wife seeking a new husband who can mean passports for her and the children. Newspaper advertisements offering Western marriages receive scores of applicants. An attractive Hong Kong woman teacher who at the age of thirty-five is an old maid by Chinese reckoning actually committed herself on the strength of what seemed a very promising offer in the advertisement columns, but was shocked to find a would-be overseas Chinese bridegroom more than twice as old as herself. Yet despite his white hair he was cultivated and considerate; after a couple of months' trial they decided to make a go of it. A rich old man who finds a pretty young bride must know what he's doing, say the cynics. With enough late-night parties, he will not keep her waiting too long to inherit.

What about marriages on the Mainland? In the countryside of the less developed provinces, life has changed little. Where prosperity has brought more leisure a strange revolution is underway.

Husbands and wives (especially wives) are asking what married life holds for them, looking for new answers, questioning accepted attitudes.

A large-scale little-publicized change of thinking is underway in the cities. In some ways it reflects the disputes between factions in the governing establishment, between traditional attitudes and the demand for the enjoyments life can offer.

You can read articles which seem to disparage the earlier teachings of Chairman Mao and discourage women from entering the professions and forging their own careers. Instead a much more old-fashioned figure is being quietly promoted — the good, long-suffering wife and mother, the self-sacrificing heroine who accepts a harsh fate for the sake of others. No Ibsen personality here, seeking self-fulfilment. The girl Huifang, heroine in the Mainland TV series Expectations, is the proclaimed model. Scriptwriters and directors have been quick to imitate. These characters win social respect, says an official commentator, because they have sacrificed their own happiness and endured humiliations while shouldering family and other responsibilities.

"For instance, a young widow would accept a young man's marriage proposal only after he had agreed to take care of her first mother-in-law; or a young woman would only divorce her lunatic husband if her new lover allowed her former husband to live with them; and another middle-aged woman remained single all her life for the sake of her social and family duties."

The most celebrated of these female creations is Li Shulan, in the opera *There Lives a Daughter-in-Law within the Gate*. Her husband divorces her and goes away to the city, sending her money every month to take care of his elderly parents and the young son. Li Shulan, a simple country girl, bears no grudge against the husband, cares for his parents, sees the son through college without touching any of her husband's money, and refuses other men's courtship to avoid gossip. Twenty years later Li finds her husband and returns his remittances. He offers remarriage but meets with a dignified refusal.

These portrayals of women recently aroused lively debate on the Mainland. Some cities praised the traditional female virtues shown by a simple countrywoman, others deplored the playwright's so-called "feudal return to the past".

Mainland Chinese women are told that they "hold up half the sky" and are respectfully treated in Party propaganda, but too often freedom for the wife simply means that she can go out to earn money — while also looking after the household as before. Women rarely reach top positions and find it difficult to

It is a well known fact that all Chinese girls, however homely before and after, always appear radiantly beautiful on their wedding days.

secure redress when abused by officialdom. Only one woman is a minister in today's mainland government. Women prominent in recent years have nearly always been the wives of well-known men, exercising reflected power.

Yet, although they have often had to fight their way as second-rate citizens, women in China show themselves capable of extraordinary efforts and play an impressive role in social and professional life, as teachers, doctors and nurses, and they also work in factories, in the fields and down the mines. And away from the Mainland — in Hong Kong, Singapore and other overseas communities — they suffer far less discrimination and sometimes make their presence felt politically.

On the Mainland big changes in the lives of married couples began with the economic reform encouraged by patriarch Deng Xiaoping. They are the sequel to earlier, unsuccessful moves to make married women's lives easier.

Almost, you might feel, the ups and downs of modern China, beginning with the victory of the Communists in 1949, have been mirrored in the way women have been treated, their chances of happiness in work, marriage and family life.

In his younger days Chairman Mao Zedong was much concerned with justice for women and wrote powerful polemics over the untimely death of a certain Miss Zhao, betrothed without her consent to a son of the influential Wu family. Miss Zhao's dislike of the idea of marriage to Mr. Wu was so intense that she slit her throat in the red sedan

The bride's wrists and hands are loaded with gold. The dress is of floral design and colour, with red predominating.

chair carrying her to her fiancé's home for the wedding ceremony. The two families then quarrelled over the cost of burying her. Mao spoke out strongly against the "shameful system of arranged marriages" and one of the first measures brought in by the Communists after 1949 was a marriage law to establish equal rights for women and make it easier for them to obtain divorces. As a result life did become more bearable for many Chinese women, though some clumsy local officials caused suicides by bullying women into divorces they didn't want, just to produce more impressive statistics.

However the pattern of married life changed little for many years. Professional women were expected to reserve their love for Chairman Mao and the revolution and actually to welcome a chance to work a thousand miles away from their husbands if the Party and Marxist-Leninism-Mao-Thought so ordained. As for couples left together, here of course the wives could enjoy greater freedom — go out to work and not bother with the housework until they got home at night and cooked and cleared away the supper. The husband might lend a hand, once children arrived. Certainly in a marriage like that a woman wouldn't feel she was idle or ornamental.

Then in 1978 began China's economic reforms and, according to Mainland official writers, they affected the lives of married couples so suddenly that they were almost taken off their guard. Many city households now had refrigerators and washing machines. Income was no longer a matter of pooling two lots of wages to support the family. A single parent now had enough money to bring up a child. Husbands and wives began to ask whether marriage shouldn't mean something much more than down-to-earth partnership and some were unable to find the answer to an unexpressed longing for happiness.

In 1979 there were 320,000 divorces in Mainland China. In 1988 it was more than double — 650,000. Attitudes towards extramarital love affairs have changed. Five years ago a survey showed most people deploring relationships outside the marriage but two years ago respondents mostly said they were not sure.

Strangely, the word "love" began to appear in written debates on successful marriage. Men and women began advertising in the papers with descriptions of the kind of partner they were seeking and also saying what they thought they could contribute to a marriage.

"Marriage no longer meant simply living together, cooking and bearing children," says the Mainland monthly *China Today*. Engels' dictum, that a marriage without love was a marriage without morality, was frequently quoted.

"Advertisements in newspapers and magazines began to change too. Women requested men who were 'handsome, honourable and open-minded'. Men asked for women who were 'gentle and refined, with elegant bearing' and 'beautiful both inside and outside'."

In 1990 Beijing Television Station launched a matchmaking programme: *Tonight We Meet* in which men and women seeking a spouse actually presented themselves on the screen. The TV director said: "The programme not only provides opportunities for single men and women, but also tries to smash the trammels of old feudal ideas that are obstacles to happiness, helping to create completely new views on life, love and marriage."

A woman journalist came on the programme to declare that whereas in the past it was always the wife who must be pure and virtuous, the men ought to be virtuous husbands and fathers, to play their part in creating a family that would be "relaxed and harmonious, understanding and faithful".

Chapter 8

Love, Sex, and Homosexuality

Sex is very big business these days. The *Hong Kong Telephone Buying Guide* has a dozen illustrated pages of female escorts and male masseurs. The clientele is partly visiting businessmen and women but a local prostitution clientele has mushroomed with the emergence of a rich upper-middle class, a new race of tough, vigorous business entrepreneurs who've made a heap of money and whose tastes are basic.

Organization is in the hands of the Triads (known as the black society). Promising recruits are good-looking girls in their middle and late teens who, though they still live at home, do what they like because their parents are both working and hardly see their children.

"People with pretty daughters have plenty to worry about," said a Hong Kong teacher. "They know that rich

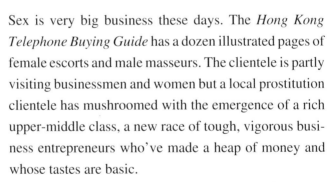

Advertisement for "Room to be rented by the hour", "Acupressure" and "Massage" are displayed along Mong Kok streets. The police have been cracking down on brothels.

Motel in a main road in Kowloon Tong. All is discreet, well conducted.

men are ready to pay enormous sums for the particular kind of girl that suits their fantasy. She can become very rich in no time at all — drive around in a Rolls Royce."

A prosperous businessman will contact a young starlet and say "Be mine exclusively for three months, and I will pay you a million dollars." The phrase for this procedure is "*baoqilai*" — the words you use for booking a room in a restaurant. "The offer is usually much higher than that," commented a film-worker. "A million dollars is the absolute minimum. Of course he does have the girl exclusively. There is so much money splashing around. The developers have most of it. They live in flats with gold taps in the bathrooms, while ordinary people can scarcely afford a roof over their heads because of all the inflation in flat-prices."

Prostitution shows many faces in Hong Kong (as in all big international cities) but what worries social workers most is its growing prevalence among

Club BBOSS is a centre of attraction for tourists and official visitors. In many clubs hostesses may be hired out.

teenagers. A schoolgirl gets paid five hundred dollars for selling herself to a client for an afternoon. The Triad go-betweens take three hundred of it. In a court case last year it was revealed that a schoolgirl had a pager in class for receiving details of rendezvous with waiting clients.

Extramarital sex in Hong Kong is a garden of many pavilions. "Lots of affairs going on," said a British Army wife a few years ago. "But if it comes to light, you've had it. You're posted away at very short notice."

"Romance is all right," said an elderly lady from Shanghai (She had once been very beautiful), "but for that a man needs money and a lot of spare time. No lack of cash here but, apart from some obvious exceptions, people don't seem to have the time for sensational affairs. Too busy making more money, I suppose."

Another lady said, recalling old days: "You may decry the idea of concubines or secondary wives, but sometimes I think there was some wisdom

The well-known Jazz Club at Lan Kwai Fong where couples drink and listen to music.

in it. If your husband wants that sort of thing when you've had enough and feel past it, why not let him have some young woman? Saves a lot of trouble and frustration."

A good-looking overweight man in a well-cut suit and silk tie said having an affair was one hell of a business because Hong Kong is such a small place; and it's no use thinking of Macau, because you run into people there just as much.

An elderly Chinese professional man confessed: "When I was young boys were brought up not to know about sex. Despite all the talk about sex education in schools, we are still a very inhibited society. Chinese couples can marry and have children and grow old and die without ever understanding the exquisite pleasures arising from romantic and physical contacts."

Nowadays visits to girlie-bars are often seen as a necessary part of commercial life. The potential customer expects an evening on the town, including a nightclub with hostesses who can be hired out. A woman night club manageress said: "Men used to come here on their own, for female companionship to brighten their lives after a disappointing day. Now they come in quartets — local managers bringing foreign customers."

"Communists from the Mainland never used to come but now they do, and always in groups, so they can keep an eye on each other."

In the earlier decades of the People's Republic, Mainland China prided itself on its sexual purity. "One thing we don't suffer from," a Guangzhou surgeon proudly told me, a visiting journalist back in 1972, "is your Western venereal diseases." And indeed the Mainland record of rehabilitating prostitutes and generally eradicating sexual exploitation in China's cities was

Young lovers ignore the Hong Kong world of concrete, profit, and overcrowding.

impressive. "We have no prostitutes," the surgeon added.

They certainly do now. The authorities, waking up to what is seen officially as a serious and growing social problem, have been enforcing harsh measures, especially in the coastal provinces where prosperity has changed the lives of many.

In Guangdong province next to Hong Kong raids have been stepped up on hotels, beauty parlours and dance clubs. In one police operation more than 7,000 prostitutes and their customers were arrested.

Recently a number of Hong Kong businessmen, caught in a raid in the Special Economic Zone of Shenzhen, were sent off to labour camps for four months. The Special Economic Zones are notorious. They are said to bring the girls from faraway, from the far Northwest, to minimize the danger of AIDS. This is represented in official propaganda as an evil entering China from abroad and prostitutes offering their services to foreigners have come in for specially severe punishment. A few pimps and brothel-keepers have been executed as an example to the rest.

"Why is it?" sighed a Mainland Chinese social worker, "that when we open up to Western influence we always seem to adopt the worst things in your culture?"

"All this rubbish about sex has caused endless problems," grumbled a conservatively brought-up old man from the North. "It is all this Western stuff, these romantic novels and films about women unable to choose between husband and lover and sacrificing themselves for passion. We call that 'yellow culture' because of the colour of mud at the bottom of the swamp."

That is very much the older generation talking. Other men and women with experience of life in China will point out that, although Western literature and films have presented human feelings and longings in a more overt way, love and desire and hate and the agony of parting have been known in China (and for thousands of years) just as strongly as in the West.

"It's just that we haven't been in the habit of making such a display of our feelings," as a young Chinese wife said. "But if you read Chinese poetry and classics like the *Dream of the Red Chamber*, you'll be left in little doubt about the state of affairs from earliest times."

Two years ago the Hong Kong Government decriminalized homosexual relationships between consenting adults in private. It was a measure long overdue. Attitudes towards homosexuality have changed worldwide over the years (though it is still a crime in Mainland China) and a more enlightened environment in Hong Kong has caused a whole poisonous atmosphere of blackmail and persecution to be cleaned out. Well within living memory men in important posts have been prevented from proceeding against wrongdoers by the threat of being reported to the police for homosexual tendencies.

There are many conservatives in Hong Kong who claim that homosexuality is a pathological condition unknown among the Chinese, despite the evidence to the contrary in Chinese classical literature. There is anyway not the same public interest in the question as elsewhere. A "gay" week due to be held here to celebrate the anniversary of decriminalization had to be abandoned due to lack of support.

Chapter 9

Death and Funerals

To the Westerner the Chinese funeral parlour seems a strangely cold and comfortless place. Tiled anterooms, lifts, a distant clamour of a Chinese band scaring devils away, impersonal attendants. Not at all the consoling background of church and organ music and respectful, quiet men in black in the tree-girt cemetery hallowed and beloved in Christendom. Those raised in the Church of England may set foot within church doors only on occasions of baptism, marriage and death but they set great store by its sa-

The Hungry Ghosts Festival lasts for three days on Peng Chau island. It commemorates a plague which carried off most of the islanders a century ago.

Family and clan members at a village funeral.

cred atmosphere. Whereas, a funeral in Hong Kong …

Don't, however, make the mistake of thinking that death and its accompanying rituals are unimportant to the Chinese. They loom very large indeed in Chinese minds, which are much concerned with an appropriate farewell to the departing and their welfare in the next world. No invitations to the funeral are needed. It is the great occasion when friends, nearest and dearest, and also the most distant relatives will come without asking, even though they have no means of knowing how deeply the central figure appreciates their respect.

If for some reason you're unable to attend the funeral of your Chinese friend, go to the funeral hall the day before and sign the book of condolence, order flowers to be added to the great crush of blooms, mainly chrysanthemums, spread round the walls.

Chinese people traditionally associate flowers with death. They will not usually give flowers to each other as presents although Western attitudes are more often met than formerly. A Chinese friend visiting a Westerner in

A family member of the deceased watches over the coffin.

hospital may bring flowers because it's known this gives special pleasure, but they are more likely to take a practical view and choose fruit, or carefully cooked food. If the patient is seriously ill, it's very bad form indeed to bring flowers because of their relevance to funerals.

Funeral procedures vary greatly. Many families, especially the more conservative, will hire a hall in one of the large local funeral parlours and (on the day before the burial) the family members sit there by the coffin and receive the condolences of relatives, friends and colleagues. The family wear sackcloth robes of white unbleached material — colour is absent. Some families, especially Christians, wear black.

The family mourners stay there through the night, then next day they set out for the cemetery or the crematorium.

More and more Chinese families are turning to cremation. Largely it's a question of expense. You have no grave to visit at festival time, instead you will pay for a so-called shrine board in a house of worship (an ordinary house adapted for the purpose) where numbers of boards inscribed with the names of the dead are on the wall behind an altar. A married couple may share a shrine board. When one partner alone survives, red cloth or paper covers part of the board to represent the living and book ahead the space which will be needed in due course.

When families want a grave they buy it from the authorities. The body is allowed to stay there for six years before being disinterred and the bones placed in an urn. An appropriate grave site is found with the aid of a *feng shui* (geomancy) expert, and may cost the family thousands of dollars. It is mainly the older generation who feel that life after death is a kind of physical reincarnation for which the body of this life must be properly prepared in a whole and cleansed state. They resist any new ideas of bodily organs being donated to help the living.

Graves are of enormous importance. When well chosen and auspiciously situated they will confer great benefits on succeeding generations. There is a common belief in Hong Kong that the excellent siting of the family grave of Sir Y. K. Pao's forbears cast a golden glow over the great ship-owner's fortunes.

To desecrate a grave, on the other hand, is to pronounce a curse. It is rumoured among common folk that the family grave of former Chinese Premier Zhao Ziyang was mysteriously vandalized not long before he fell into disgrace over the Tiananmen democracy movement and subsequent shootings of June, 1989.

Traditionally the Chinese believe that the future life is vaguely approximate to the one they know here on earth, and well within living memory it has been the custom in some parts of China to bury clothes and valuable jewels with the dead. Back in the time of the Spring and Autumn period it is recorded that the body of Wu Gong, ruler of the State of Chin, was buried along with sixty-six retainers who were killed in order to continue in his service beyond the grave. And in 150 B.C. the First Emperor ordered that his entire household,

When night falls on the last day of the festival they ceremonially burn a tall effigy of the King of Ghosts. This, with the offerings of the dead, ensures that no ghosts will trouble the living in the year ahead.

including women and servants, should all be killed and buried with him. It is not known whether these orders were carried out, because the tomb has not yet been fully uncovered; it was perhaps an act of enlightenment that resulted in thousands of terra cotta warriors being buried as bodyguards, instead of flesh and blood soldiers.

The idea of providing for the deceased in the next world is still respected here in Hong Kong but in a more symbolic way. Paper consumer goods and paper money are burned, which is a way of translating them to the next world. They may well include a complete mah-jong set, furniture, a TV set — even a credit card, all in paper. Certain shops in Kowloon specialize in making them.

A family member explains that "while you are preparing these objects — folding up the paper money and the rest of it — your thoughts are concentrated on the dead." His sister added there are other customs which have the same intention, however child-like they may seem to the ignorant outsider. "For instance for a month after the funeral we abstain from eating beef, because according to legend the dead are conducted into the next world by monsters working for the king of the underworld, and one of them resembles a bull and this creature would make the dead suffer if we were seen eating his flesh. We are also to abstain from washing our hair for a month after the funeral because if this were observed from beyond the grave our dear departed would be forced, in the next world, to drink our shampoo-water."

"Absurd, you may say? I assure you, not to wash your hair for a month makes you think a lot about the person for whose sake you are observing this rule — especially if it all happens in the hot summer days."

A young daughter said that when her much-loved father passed away some years ago she included, among the paper next-world possessions to be burned, a letter from herself in which she begged him to get in touch with her from the next world, no matter by what means. "I was young and thought it might happen," she said. "However I got no message, nothing came. Or perhaps I lacked the means to interpret it."

The actual burial or cremation is likely to be attended only by the family, especially if it is a weekday. Hong Kong people are busy at work; they cannot

Feast of the Hungry Ghosts (in the Hungry Ghosts Festival) on Ping Chau island. Food offerings, collected by Taoist monks, placate the spirits of victims of accidents and sudden epidemics.

easily take time off.

The form of funeral services is decided by the wealth of the bereaved family, their degree of Westernization, the fame of the deceased. Well-known colleagues in commerce or government may act as pallbearers, eulogies are spoken. The dead lies in a glass-lidded coffin before a large portrait placed on the altar among the flowers and large-character names of the donors. Each new arrival signs the condolence book and bows three times to the portrait of the dead before greeting the family. And the hall will be filled. Large attendance at a funeral gives face to the bereaved.

As a Westerner you may be amazed at all the people your late Chinese friend frequented, whom you have never met before today. You thought you knew him so well. You recall exchanges of confidence, of experiences survived, of attitudes to life. He enlarged your knowledge of Chineseness. But now at the time of final parting you realize, seeing the crowded rows of strange faces, that for him you represented only one stage in a long journey

Specially folded paper money, TV sets, credit cards and motor cars are all burned, to be used by the deceased in the next world.

that began in some faraway Mainland province, included all kinds of connections and contacts in days of struggle, many sponsors and backers and protégés, friendships developed along the way, all part of a Chinese world you knew nothing about and could never share. You look at all those serious Chinese faces and wonder what brings them here, what groups they represent, what he meant to them. To outsiders, funerals of Chinese friends can really be sad events.

The body is wheeled away out of the hall, for burial or cremation, accompanied on each side by the pallbearers. At some stage the mourners are each given a coin and a sweet in a small envelope — a kind of ritual act of thanks for their attendance — and sometimes a small handkerchief to wipe away tears.

Not so long ago it would be said that the various funeral and burial services had the one strong underlying motive — reverence for ancestors, the basis of a whole Chinese system of ethics. Among simple people it was also believed that dreadful punishments awaited those who behaved badly in this life. For

The lights are lit. The food offerings have been spiritually consumed by the dead, now they can be taken home to materially fortify the living.

them Hell has eighteen separate layers. The lowest — the eighteenth — is reserved for children who kill their parents and for wives who kill their husbands (It's less serious for a husband to kill his wife; that may be just an unfortunate minor lapse). From the eighteenth hell there is no hope of salvation, no chance to repent and win some form of reincarnation. You are done for. When you next visit the Tiger Balm Garden you can see the various punishments awaiting the evildoer.

A new generation takes a light-hearted — not to say contemptuous — view of much of this folklore. Nowadays — at least in Hong Kong — the emphasis in the time of mourning is more on the solidarity of the family. Last rites must be attended by family members however remote the relationship.

"Along with weddings and important birthdays and other celebrations," says a Chinese professional man, "they are occasions when we have to postpone any other engagements and put in an appearance. You have no idea how membership of a large family takes up a man's time. But then the family is the world in which the personality finds its expression."

Chapter 10

Joys of Eating

If you tell a Chinese you don't like Chinese food he will simply write you off. If you express keen enjoyment and interest and ask questions about what the various dishes consist of, he will rather approve of you.

It's very rare to meet Westerners who can't stand Chinese food. It's possible to dislike some particular dish but not the whole range of all the extraordinary menus. Hong Kong has many restaurants where you eat as well as (or better than) in most cities of the world.

Dim sum—literally small hearts or tidbits— are small dumplings stuffed with meats and vegetables. Hard to stop eating.

Chinese cuisine here includes Cantonese, Beijing, Shanghai, Sichuan, Hangzhou, Hunan, Hakka, Teochew as well as Mongolian hotpot. Vegetarian food is delicious, especially that served in monasteries and nunneries. Nothing is more enjoyable than an evening spent eating with Chinese friends. They show the kind of good manners which aims at putting Western guests entirely at their ease.

"Use your spoon," they beg the visitor who makes a mess of chopsticks. "Actually we Chinese don't handle chopsticks very well," said the Chinese man rapidly coming to the rescue of the English girl who had dropped her chicken's foot into the soya sauce.

You may say that is carrying politeness rather far, but a Chinese friend will assure you that, in fact, numbers of Chinese people manage chopsticks very clumsily. "They've never been taught," says a local secretary. "Now, my mother was very strict about it when we were young. One chopstick held firmly against the fold between thumb and first finger. That one stays immovable. And the other you hold between first-and-second fingers and the rest so you can move it. Chopsticks have to be held two-thirds of the way up from the thin end. Children are told that if they hold the chopsticks too high up they'll have to marry someone from very faraway and if too near the thin end, then it's marriage to somebody too close, like the ugly girl next door." There is also the belief, among some Chinese friends, that if you hold your chopsticks high, you're pretending to be a high official or a very important person.

To be invited out to dinner is one of the early experiences of contact with Chinese people. You may find that, if you are the guest of the evening, your seat at the large round table is the one facing the doorway with your back to the wall. This ensures that some assassin cannot make a quick entry, plant a dagger between your shoulder blades and vanish. So often in Chinese history, it is laughingly explained, the man they wish to dispose of is given a large dinner — which he will not live to see the end of.

Quite a number of Chinese people in Hong Kong say they have never heard of this guest-back-to-the-wall custom. But everyone agrees with the basic rule of hospitality here — that the guest can do no wrong. However he or she

Chinese friends demonstrate the use of chopsticks and the Westerner should manage well enough at the second or third attempt.

behaves, it is all right with the host.

As for correct etiquette at the table, different Chinese hold different opinions. A man from North China declared there was no such thing; you just all sat down and enjoyed yourselves. However his wife, from a Guangdong family, recalled very severe discipline around the family table in childhood days. You were not supposed to reach out across the table to choose tasty morsels you specially fancied (This particular sin is known as doing a flying elephant); if you did, you would soon qualify for a rap on the head with a chopstick. You were also expected to finish up every single grain of rice in your bowl. Every grain left over would cause another pimple on your face.

A member of an old Hong Kong family insists that "at a Chinese dinner you must never ask for anything. Not as in Britain where it's quite all right to say, 'Please pass me the salt.'" And because the guests don't ask for anyone to pass them anything, this throws a heavy responsibility on the hostess, who must

The secret is to hold one chopstick rigid and adjust the other to hold tight the morsel of food desired. Hold the chopsticks about two-thirds of the way up.

watch with the eye of a hawk to make sure all the guests get just what they need for complete enjoyment.

"As a result my wife hates entertaining in our own flat," he explained, "that's why it's so much easier to have the dinner in a restaurant, where there are waiters to watch over things."

However another Chinese acquaintance said he had not heard of this "never ask for anything" etiquette, though you obviously would not pick over the food to choose a succulent morsel for yourself.

Westerners are sometimes warned against wrong-doing with regard to fish. They are told that never, when fish has been served and the top half eaten, so that only the big bone and bottom half still bask in the juice, must you turn it over to get at what remains. This would signal the ill-fortune of a ship turning belly up. You must take out your helping from beneath the bone without upheaval. Another school of thought maintains that you can turn the fish, but it must be done in one smooth movement. Making a clumsy mess is what brings bad luck.

Anyway the host will probably take care of such delicate operations. And if he uses his own chopsticks in serving you all, you must just overlook this unhygienic aspect of the care he takes of his guests. In some of Hong Kong's smarter hotel-restaurants the waiters will divide the fish for the guests using "public chopsticks" thus avoiding embarrassment for foreigners. However Chinese eating with Chinese rarely bother about this. Sharing is expected among friends. In the West, so they have heard, true lovers even share a toothbrush.

In former days Chinese wives never accompanied their husbands out to dinner in tea houses and restaurants. Men's enjoyments were a world apart. They would get together to eat and drink and there might be women to provide entertainment, but the wives stayed at home. In the Chinese world there has traditionally been a much deeper separation between the life of home and the world of companions, wine, opium and sex; but now that tradition has undergone change.

Wives often accompany their husbands; the whole structure of the family is different. What the Westerner may find strange is that, whether at banquets or casual dinners, Chinese men very often sit side-by-side with their own wives. This is so even at Western style dinners, when the wife can speak perfectly good English and converse intelligently on her own.

Chinese dinners are enlivened with short toasts. The British, unlike people on the Continent of Europe, have a dreary habit of just drinking their wine without word or ceremony as soon as it's poured. In Chinese company the host proposes a toast to start things going and you all drink together; and when you want to drink again you should raise your glass to the host and hostess and drink to them, with some appropriate compliment.

Chinese people think Westerners are very heavy drinkers and find plenty of evidence in Hong Kong to reinforce this view. Not that Chinese men are puritanically abstinent. Great poets from China's past have written their best work when drunk and everyone knows how one of the finest poets of the Tang dynasty — Li Bai — died when, after happy hours with the bottle he saw the Lady Moon reflected in the flooded rice paddy, tried to embrace her, fell in and was drowned. What a great way to go!

"In fairness to Western businessmen," said a Chinese merchant, "it must be said they usually avoid the really hard stuff and stick to whisky, wine and beer, whereas the Chinese are liable to pour out cognac or mao tai by the glassful. And when a business deal hangs on the right relaxed atmosphere you can't really say you prefer lime juice. However there are various techniques for evading the joyful call of *"Gan bei"* ("Empty the glass! Bottoms up!"). Closely watching the late Premier Zhou Enlai at a Beijing banquet one would notice how his lips always just touched the rim of the glass; he never drank a drop.

Chinese men do get drunk, at moments of elation or despair, but alcoholism is nothing like the social problem it is in, for instance, Britain or other parts of North Europe. Most Chinese women neither drink nor smoke — does this explain their flawless complexions? However both sexes drink quantities of tea — Chinese tea, taken without milk or sugar, one of the most satisfying and refreshing liquids on earth once you get into the habit.

There are at least fifty varieties of Chinese tea in any tea shop worthy the name. The most popular red tea is Pu Erh and the most favoured green tea is the Jasmine. Pu Erh is dark and on the strong side whereas the Jasmine is light and very refreshing. The strongest tea is the Tieguanyin of Fujian, taken in tiny cups and guaranteed to keep you awake and talking all night.

When the host replenishes the cups, Cantonese guests tap their fingers on the table, symbolizing the kowtow — knocking your head on the floor to show the profoundest respect. The gesture is convenient — conversation is not interrupted by thankyous to whoever is pouring out. This is a southern custom, unknown elsewhere in China and it's not done for wine, only for tea.

When in a restaurant the pot is empty and needs more hot water you simply leave the lid askew on the pot to show it's empty, and the waiter refills without asking. I was told that according to a story dating from the time of the Mongols there used to be trouble when troops from the garrison would ask for hot water

Tea is taken seriously. Hong Kong has special shops where experts tell you about the many varieties and how to prepare and enjoy them.

on the tea but put a mouse or cockroach in the pot and make this the excuse for causing trouble. And once, it is said, a customer put his pet budgerigar in the empty pot for warmth and the waiter, not seeing it, killed it with scalding water. When the lid was already tilted the waiter could see in and check there were no foreign objects.

When it comes to food the Cantonese readily admit that they are the true gourmets, the connoisseurs, the creative artists.

As any Chinese housewife will tell you, food must be bought when it's absolutely fresh. That means a daily visit to the market by the amah or her mistress. "And what I want you to understand," said our neighbour the evening we were invited, "is that this fish you are eating was bought when it was still alive. Not just frozen but alive and healthy. So it simply could not do you more good." We were duly impressed.

Chinese deride the West for not making better use of all that heaven offers us from the animal and vegetable world. They are proud of the skill and cunning with which full use is made of all the parts of animals, all the kinds of fish, all the vegetable life, in the production of unforgettably tasty dishes. We know the various sayings about the Cantonese interest in food — that they will eat anything that flies as long as it isn't an aeroplane and anything that moves on the ground provided it's not a car or a bicycle.

You might say this is exaggerated, but it is true they use entrails and other parts of animals the Western cook discards and from these produce wonderful dishes. The main principle of Chinese cooking is that it takes a deal of time and trouble to prepare — cutting up and mixing, marinating and soaking in wine and sauces — and is cooked very quickly, usually in that large shallow metal dish called a *wok*, and then served in small pieces, easy to digest. This may be the reason why, after even a large and prolonged Chinese dinner, you rarely leave with a feeling of having eaten too much.

But a Chinese man admitted that the first time he was invited to a Western meal he had a shock. Nothing more daunting, he said, than a steak, a large chunk of bleeding meat. And the soup came first as a barely significant overture, rather out of place.

Because soup, for many Chinese — especially when at home — is often a magnificent climax to a meal. "You put anything and everything into it," said a young housewife. "And you simmer it for hours. It's wonderful in the cold weather; you can put medicine in with it to keep your family healthy and when you add specially tasty ingredients it keeps your husband home in the evenings."

There's a growing taste for hot-pot in Hong Kong, especially in the cold weather when vegetable prices soar. In your central pot is Tientsin cabbage, fishballs, beefballs, bean curd; you sit around, select bits of raw meat (lamb, beef, chicken, fish slices, but never pork) and hold them in the boiling liquid for twenty seconds or so before eating.

This kind of meal has become popular in Hong Kong even in the summer. There are special hot-pot restaurants which keep the temperature down with air-conditioning.

In the cold months you can eat snake. Snake banquets have become popular, with all the courses, including the soup, made from snake ingredients. In fact the meat in the soup is often only a quarter snake and the rest chicken. It's supposed to be very good for the eyes. Eat snake regularly they say, and you will never need glasses.

The gall-bladders of certain snakes are very good cures for arthritis and rheumatism. The more poisonous the snake the more effective. A friend was recently in the city of Wuzhou in Guangxi province where they kill and pack the snakes for despatch to Hong Kong. There are complaints about cheating. Some of the snakes are less poisonous than they are made out to be.

You might well think that, once having been introduced to Chinese cooking, whether the endless variety of Cantonese dishes, the refinements of Shanghai, the hot chilli flavourings of Sichuan or fortifying dumplings of the north, the Westerner will never want to return to the bangers and mash and homely meals that mother used to make or the French and Italian dishes of Western restaurants. Yet strangely enough, after a week or two in China with nothing but Chinese food for breakfast, lunch and dinner, the Western palate does tend to long for the cooking it was brought up on. A question of metabolism, or sheer digestive conservatism. An unvarying breakfast of congee (rice porridge) can be a specially trying ordeal to those reared on

Fingers tapping on the table convey respectful thanks— kowtow—without interrupting the flow of talk.

orange juice, choice of two eggs with sausages, ham or bacon, followed by toast and marmalade and unlimited replenishments of coffee.

A strange phenomenon is the young Chinese businessman who after travel in Europe is converted to the relative simplicities of Western cooking. He buys a microwave cooker, studies Western recipes. And his wife has changed with him, won over by his willingness to do all the cooking himself.

It is, when all's said and done, merely a matter of taste and temperament. I am no gourmet, but I find almost nothing to compete with the early Cantonese lunch of dim sum (little hearts) — tiny dumplings filled with vegetable and meat, washed down with unlimited quantities of Jasmine tea.

The Chinese agree with Dr. Johnson — that if a man is not interested in what goes into his stomach, he is unlikely to be interested in anything else. A usual form of greeting all over China is: "Have you eaten yet?" — with the unspoken corollary that if you are uncultured enough to say no, you haven't, you are likely to be dragged into the next restaurant.

"If, at the end of a day's work, we can't enjoy a tasty, well-cooked meal, then life simply isn't worth living," is how a local food-columnist sums it up. First in life comes food, then shelter, then money and security, then the cultural frills. A simple man who by hard work and a measure of luck has made a vast fortune, takes quiet satisfaction in the thought that he has made enough to feed the family for the next four or five generations.

"We are peasants at heart," said a Chinese business friend, "that explains why we attach such importance to food. In our collective memory is the joy of a good harvest, the dreadful silence in the village in the time of famine."

His wife said: "We take food seriously and that is one of the reasons why I don't like your cocktail parties which are a completely Western custom. Partly it's a feeling of shyness many Chinese undergo when they find themselves among complete strangers. But eating all those tidbits in a wasteful, absent-minded way while you stand around and talk — the idea is very alien to us."

"But you have dim sum, which are also small and delicious?"

"Then we sit down at a table to enjoy them and take seriously what we are eating. I would like to see all cocktail parties abolished."

But the more Westernized Chinese accept the custom. Drinks parties, they agree, are useful for entertaining large numbers of people, launching new publications, saying goodbye to a colleague, maintaining business contacts. Western influences are insidious. "All those schoolchildren with their fat bodies," exclaimed a Chinese mother. "It's disgusting. They used to eat rice and vegetables at midday and that was a good healthy diet. Now it's off to MacDonald's for hot dogs and hamburgers. No wonder they're overweight."

When one Westerner rings up another to take him out to lunch, it's expected that whoever telephones, invites and books the table will also foot the bill.

According to Chinese friends, no such convention exists in their culture. Never mind who has taken the initiative, all this means is agreeing to have lunch together at a certain time and place. Hence the need, at the end of the meal, to decide who is going to pay. And because face comes into it — the one who foots the bill considers it an honour to be able to pay — sometimes it comes to pushing and shoving, verging on a fight.

Chapter 11

China
Communism
Inc.

Since 1978 when Deng Xiaoping opened the door to economic reform China has been the scene of big city enterprises, millions of small new factories, unemployment among the farmers and sometimes golden rewards for local and outside entrepreneurs.

It has changed Mainland China and changed Hong Kong. For many it has seemed more far-reaching in its effects than the Communist take-over of 1949. For it corresponds more closely than socialism ever could to the essential pragmatism of the Chinese temperament.

It has not been all plain sailing. Great optimism in the early 1980s gave way to acute disappointment as inflation soared, panic-buying emptied the shops and students and workers demonstrated against racketeering and graft. Impatient foreign entrepreneurs burned their fingers.

The square of the railway station at Shenzhen, one of the Mainland's Special Economic Zones where the socialist open market looks more like Hong Kong everyday.

They had expected an easy ride in China, forgetting that this was a vast Third World country largely lacking infrastructure and impeded at many levels by ignorant or self-seeking officials (so many of the better quality having been hounded to death in the Cultural Revolution).

Then conditions improved and today, despite some problems of inflation and disagreements among the leadership in Beijing over appointments to key positions, it's a case of all-systems-go, with Deng himself urging more and faster development. Make a profit and help China.

This is a message Hong Kong businessmen are delighted to hear. Hundreds of thousands of Hong Kong Chinese, Japanese, Westerners, and other entrepreneurs are making healthy and sometimes hefty profits, especially in the province of Guangdong next to Hong Kong. The whole business and industrial scene has been transformed. Hong Kong is turning into a service centre. It books the orders but the work's done across the border, at wage-levels a tenth of the colony's. Already the manufacturing work force in Guangdong province (a former farming area) is four times the size of Hong Kong's. Hong Kong orders mean three million Mainland jobs.

Hong Kong and Cantonese businessmen understand each other, speak the same language. Together they face the problems — chronic lack of electrical power, difficult customs regulations, interfering officials.

"I found it better to avoid the Special Economic Zones," says a Hong Kong director who employs five thousand people in the province. " Too much red tape there. I went to an upland village (on a motor bike because there was no road, only a track) and talked to the elders. We set up our first assembly plant in a hall used for storing grain. Took the girls off the fields, promised them clean toilets and a clean canteen. Paid them three hundred Hong Kong dollars a month which was ten times what they could earn locally — though a tenth of Hong Kong levels — and they were delighted. That was five or six years ago. Now you might have to bargain more but it's still a promising scene."

More American firms are entering China. Losses and frustration still wait for those who miscalculate through impatience or ignorance of local conditions, but the risks are worth taking.

These days both the Chinese and the Westerners know each other much better than before and the newcomer has an easier time. The Mainland is more aware of the world outside.

Old prejudices and habits of distrust survive vigorously, however. Westerners may get better service in restaurants and trains but run into unexpected obstruction from local regulations suddenly revealed. A kind of political schizophrenia persists.

How far is business with the foreigner affected? It's the usual odd equation embracing elemental distrust of foreigners and Chinese traditional politeness and hospitality. At least visiting business teams need not fear bleak unfriendliness on arrival — far from it. From the first encounter at the airport by the reception committee smiling courtesy abounds. Sometimes a reception room is rented for the guests to rest in while formalities are completed and the transport brought round. Usually everything goes briskly; the hosts understand very well the fatigues and jet-lag of the long flight.

Certain general principles prevail. From the beginning — from the time when the visit to China is first planned — a great deal will obviously depend on the type and scale of the project. The foreigners may represent a firm with a world reputation, and are being welcomed at the highest level, because they are bringing in know-how and technology and plan to manufacture products helpful to China's high-tech progress and export trade. Then it's top red carpet treatment. At lower levels, foreign firms who've made contacts through their trade commissioners or chambers of trade will still find their opposite numbers responsive if the scheme looks promising and mutually profitable.

Certain precautions must be observed. It is absolutely essential for the visitors to know just whom they are dealing with, what is the status of the chief negotiator on the Chinese side and how far his power runs. There have been many cases in the past of visiting negotiating teams spending weeks and months with the wrong people and being obliged to go through it all again with those they should have been dealing with in the first place.

This can sometimes be avoided, if the visitors already have representatives in China to carry out reconnaissance. Time spent in reconnaissance is seldom wasted as they used to say in army training. Wherever possible send an advance party to get the scene set and the preliminaries agreed.

The Chinese official or businessman also wants to know just who his visitor is and what authority he wields. Life in a crowded country where the main loyalty is to the family has taught Chinese to distrust all strangers. He will be reassured if the newcomer was in the same class at school or college or comes from the same neighbourhood. He will take his time over developing a friendship with a Westerner, although when mutual trust is finally created it can be a very powerful joint venture asset. Never forget, however, that if you vouch for another Westerner *vis-à-vis* your Chinese friend, this is a serious matter. If the newcomer turns out to be unreliable or crooked you really will be held responsible and your China business suffer because of it.

An important occasion is the welcoming banquet, staged by the hosts so that the two sides can come to know each other and the Western side feel relaxed (and more responsive to friendly Chinese pressures). If, during the meal, the chief Western negotiator reveals himself as a man who knows something of China and speaks with polite respect of its history and problems; if he enjoys his host's jokes as well as the food and helps establish a generally genial atmosphere, this can greatly influence the days ahead.

Business negotiations always need patience, unruffled good humour and the ability to understand another culture and another kind of logic. Sooner or later the Westerner comes to realize an attitude common not only in China but in other parts of the Far East and the developing world generally: "We are very poor and you are very rich, so please do not expect equality in this deal. You must be ready to put in far more than we can afford to do. We assume you agree with this, that you still see an outcome to these talks very profitable to yourself, otherwise you would not be here in the first place."

Following the open door policy initiated by Deng Xiaoping in 1978, many Chinese officials were showing an almost patronizing attitude towards the foreign businessmen and tourists streaming into the great Middle Kingdom. Westerners had to be ready for cavalier treatment and still be grateful.

These attitudes changed with the Tiananmen debacle of June 1989. The

Mainland China announces a powerful presence in Hong Kong with I. M. Pei's 70-storey Bank of China building.

tourists stopped coming, so did the businessmen. Quiet fell on the empty hotels, the deserted conference rooms. From now on, it was realized, China would have to do more to reassure the Westerners, stick more closely to international rules if previous links were to be reforged. The situation is now easier and conditions are much improved but problems persist.

The question of personal inducements and favours can be difficult. The Chinese authorities are continually publicizing a nationwide war on corruption; the public is urged to report cases to special bureaux. Thousands of (mostly minor) officials have been sentenced in recent campaigns.

Corruption is a serious matter both in terms of capital lost abroad through light-fingered officials and the resources spent in fighting the "evil wind." An army of 360,000 people from four ministries regularly devotes most of its time to controlling graft. Thousands of companies have been audited including some of the biggest such as China International Trust and Investment Corporation (CITIC). In a recent campaign the authorities are said to have uncovered more than 9,500 cases where government ministries had profited from contacts with a Chinese commercial organization.

Despite these efforts conditions favouring corruption in China have not greatly changed, though the aims and methods used may be more discreet and sophisticated. Nowadays you won't be asked bluntly for six Mercedes-Benz cars as "samples." Government officials (though this does not apply to their children) are categorically forbidden to take part in trade and industry.

"Irregular practices" may include a request for a sum of money to be deposited in a Hong Kong bank account. A foreigner may find the conversation turning to the question of Western education for teenage offspring of his Chinese host. If he can be helpful in securing access to some foreign school or university, by writing letters of introduction or in other ways, this may be highly appreciated. Two West European firms were recently interested in starting up enterprises in Shanghai, in the new Pudong Industrial and Business Area across the river. They failed to get the cooperation they were counting on. "We weren't on the same wavelength," a Chinese official explained to a Chinese acquaintance. " They simply didn't understand the importance, to a Chinese in a certain position, of an offer to help get his children educated in

Germany. One cannot broach these topics bluntly. It has to be done indirectly. But these foreigners simply wanted to talk business in a very stubborn and limited way."

Another Chinese businessman said: "Foreigners don't understand that these days we want other things besides money. Business is sometimes the means to an end — earning merit points by carrying out government policy, or enabling a family to emigrate. Foreigners are sometimes just too ignorant. They don't understand the human situation inside China today."

Sometimes the answer to this and kindred problems is to establish an office in Shanghai or other city intended to be the centre of operations. And this office must be staffed by Chinese who know what strings are being pulled in the business and political world, and whose support is needed. They can develop the vital contacts. They can help choose whatever local organization can best take part in a joint venture, carry out a manufacturing contract, introduce and vouch for the Westerners.

With local representation of this kind the Western firm may well find the going easier and win far more tangible advantages from, for instance, the much publicized invitation to the West to invest in the new Shanghai, with all formalities simplified.

In modern China it is still personal connections that count. The Communists, when they came to power in 1949, saw themselves as the initiators of a new revolutionary regime whose mission was to serve the masses — something new in Chinese history. But it now seems clear that, forty odd years later, it's the old traditional Chinese culture which has surprisingly prevailed against local versions of Marxism-Leninism.

Although a Western entrepreneur from the 1930s returning to China today would find many changes, he would also come across much in the mercantile scene to remind him of the old days. What would probably strike him most is a much keener enthusiasm at many levels for making money quickly. But officialdom would still be trying to cream off benefits and control the action.

Interpreters are enormously important. In China the profession is not well paid. Talents vary enormously. During difficult discussions an interpreter provided by a Chinese government department may or may not convey the

Even the sophisticated Hong Kong manufacturers are now moving factories to the Mainland because labour is so much cheaper there. Hong Kong is becoming more of a service centre.

exact weight of an argument or situation. A careless interpreter can cause serious misunderstandings.

Sometimes in the middle of negotiations the Chinese side will put on a great show of righteous anger, or sessions may be postponed several times for no apparent reason. Is this just a softening up process, or have the talks really hit a serious snag? It is important to find out. There are so many possible reasons. It may be that some other government department is muscling in on the deal, or simply trying to strangle the project (In China, there is very little liaison between government ministries and departments). Or the hold-up may be due

to some very important higher-ups wanting to think over the whole affair before proceeding to the next step. Or the same higher-ups, armed with the information and background intelligence already gleaned, are simultaneously and cold-bloodedly negotiating with another visiting delegation, in the hope of getting the project underway more economically with a different set of foreign partners. These situations put a high premium on nerves of steel and general resourcefulness. At such times the personal relationships developed in the early stages can make an enormous difference.

A hard-headed European businessman in Hong Kong, with years of experience in trading with the Mainland, says that the most important thing to decide is the moment when the whole deal has become unprofitable and a waste of time, to convey this frankly to the other side, and announce the pull-out. This may have unexpectedly happy results. Or perhaps not. The Chinese side usually have a fairly shrewd appreciation of just how much the foreigner wants to start business with them, and how far he is prepared to give way.

It's along the east and south fringe of China — the so-called Gold Coast where the Special Economic Zones enjoy favourable conditions and the foreigners used to live and trade in the former Treaty Ports — that foreign negotiators are likely to come across blind spots. Modern practices acceptable in London, Frankfurt or New York may simply not be understood. Part of good etiquette on the part of the Westerner lies in making his Chinese counterpart painlessly aware of the changes in the score without causing loss of face or resentment. As for provinces further inland and cities removed from the big centres, life is simpler and attitudes less smooth. This doesn't at all mean that negotiations are easier to handle.

"The worst scenario of all," said a Western director, "is when you come against an official who has no ambition and no real interest in your project. He just sits there tying up everything in obstruction and red tape. Such people are, I suppose, partly the result of the Cultural Revolution years, when schools and universities were closed. I am glad to say there seem to be fewer of such people about these days. Instead you can meet managers and officials in their late thirties and early forties who have been abroad on trade missions. And even if the man you deal with is unfamiliar with modern practices, that doesn't matter so long as he's enthusiastic and has faith in the project."

Problems can arise over written contracts. In fact in Chinese eyes contracts are often seen rather as general expressions of intent and joint purpose — not sets of binding conditions. They are there to be changed when circumstances change.

It is vital to be clear on this early in the negotiations; otherwise misunderstandings will almost certainly sour the project at some stage. Sometimes it's a case of: "Yes, but this contract is signed by Mr. Wang. He is no longer with us and we don't know where he has gone. We cannot really be bound by what he agreed. Perhaps it would be better if we drew up a new arrangement."

Call it flexibility or Mainland cussedness, a situation like this may crop up and need smiling patience to resolve. So much depends on the amount of confidence already achieved. And as your Chinese friends will point out, sticking inflexibly to the small print is not always the best way. Not long ago a joint venture hotel project faced disaster because the Hong Kong backers had badly miscalculated the probable returns. The Mainland side, after listening to their case, agreed without demur to draw up a fresh contract. That might not have been so easy in Europe.

The Westerner has to understand, and be prepared. He has to keep remembering that China has a short history as an industrialized country. Three quarters of the people are farmers. Many of the big manufacturing plants were introduced by the invading Japanese in the northeast provinces they occupied well within living memory. Confucius may rarely be mentioned but his teachings still go deep, and so for many Chinese words like "loyalty", "obligation", "modesty" mean for more than "efficiency", "productivity" or "profit margins".

Seniority counts for a great deal. The old factory hand won't listen to a newly promoted younger manager. The hospital nurse of age and experience won't take orders from a newly qualified doctor. The Chinese graduate who goes abroad to study management or computer theory in a Western university may well find on his return that he has no hope of a job where he can use his newly-acquired know-how. Older officials will assign him instead to a minor post in a remote area. Not surprisingly the Chinese student doing well abroad may try hard to stay there.

Since 1978 the Chinese Government and various research institutes, hospitals and colleges have supported more than 90,000 students going abroad for research and study. And more than half — about 50,000 — have never returned.

All this complicates the scene for the Western firm hiring managerial staff. Many Chinese workers have been conditioned to a system where everyone gets the same wages and bonuses regardless of the amount or quality of the work they do, and even today, despite all to the talk of cleaning up and streamlining the loss-making state-run industries, the inefficient cannot be sacked without a good deal of red tape.

A man or woman who wins promotion because of proven ability, rather than seniority, is often the target of envy and disapproval. This applies especially to the state-run industries but joint ventures are not exempt. Some Western directors find themselves simply unable to cope with this kind of situation, and quit in disgust. Their more patient competitors know the scene is changing all the time and take the long-term view.

In fact in an increasing number of joint ventures, or wholly foreign-run firms, it is becoming possible to base salaries on ability but it's still a novel concept. There are other problems. A Chinese manager is not going to reprimand a staff member if it can be avoided. He is not going to initiate new methods or suggest money-saving processes. It is much safer to say "No, it can't be done" than run the risk of showing and encouraging initiative and then suffering loss of face if a new idea fails. You may say this is a universal weakness; that indifferent management is to be found in many countries. What is special to China is that here it's related to a national temperamental outlook, cemented by centuries of tradition.

Questions of rewards and promotions are often related to training. A large foreign firm engaged in a joint venture in North China was doing so well at the end of two years that it was decided to open up new factories in two other provinces. But now the need to raise levels of skill and standardize output arose, which meant they would need a training department, headed by a training manager. The Chinese side were dead against it. There was no need for training, it would only create problems. The argument lasted weeks; until the Chinese suggested that the best thing would be to have key personnel trained in Europe. Finally they agreed to accept a training manager in the Chinese factories but without holding out much hope that he would be able to achieve anything. Results are still in doubt.

Training, to its critics, suggested a Chinese being criticized and corrected by some stranger. That just would not do. In the West you may organize a brainstorming session with heads of sections advancing ideas, contradicting and attacking each other, venting opinions and ideas in confrontational give-and-take, and (hopefully) all good friends afterwards. You could not organize such a session in a Chinese firm. Call it touchiness or sensitivity or general wariness, for two Chinese businessmen to be in loud open disagreement is inconceivable.

Despite all the problems, operating on the China Mainland has its obvious advantages. Productivity may be low largely because of the slow rhythm of operations in Chinese factories. Mainland workers coming to Hong Kong for courses found the nine-to-five programme exhausting. However given the wages differential there is still an enormous potential profit for the outside entrepreneur.

At present Deng Xiaoping and his fellow advocates of economic reform seem to be gaining ground. There is still resistance from hard-liners and the possibility of unrest among workers laid off. Discussion about the need to improve the state-owned large enterprises grows more intense. A third of them are still losing money.

And as the force of ideology slackens, more and more voices are heard saying it's time China caught up with Japan and the other newly industrializing countries. It's a situation fraught with contradictions too sharp to be resolved

Cheap, dexterous labour has shot the Far East ahead of the recession-ridden West. When it comes to assembly work, girls are best.

at the Fourteenth Party Congress, though Deng certainly seems to have got his way. One great question concerns the political control the government in Beijing is able to maintain. Is it possible for such a centralized regime to exercise effective control over twenty-six provinces and five autonomous regions containing a rapidly developing nation of twelve hundred million people? And if it becomes clear that Beijing is losing control, how will the leadership seek to regain it?

Meanwhile life has become more comfortable for many millions of Chinese people especially in the towns and cities and areas of the countryside near to Hong Kong. And when people begin to acquire consumer goods and more leisure, when a middle class is growing, then inevitably new voices are heard, asking for a say in the way life is governed. It is quite impossible to say what the effect of the Chinese economic revolution will be ten or even five years from now.

Chapter 12

Black Society

Western people in Hong Kong call them the Triads. Chinese call them the Black Society. One of the advantages Westerners enjoy in Hong Kong is that the Black Society leaves them pretty much alone, though some Western firms may pay "protection money".

What are the Triads? Triads means three — Earth, Man and Heaven — and it was originally the name of one of the secret societies which made up Hong Kong's version of the Mafia, the criminal pro-

No fuss, no threats—just a friendly warning that the Brothers know you'll be opening that new restaurant in a few weeks time, and they'll be along to discuss protection.

tection world. The Black Society! It's everything that's criminal, squalid, and inhuman, and it penetrates Hong Kong life like a poison working through the veins.

Claims have been made at various times that the Triads have been split up and largely suppressed, but they always survive. Thirty years ago a Western journalist working in Hong Kong might well hear the occasional story of Triad activity — restaurant-owners mauled with meat-choppers because they failed to pay "protection", fights between rival gangs over territory, police appeals to the public to come forward with information. But if the journalist suggested a write-up, head office were likely to turn him down, because it had all been covered so often before.

Yet the story refuses to die. It enjoys, strangely enough, a positive beginning. The early secret societies were patriotic. Their members were dedicated to the defence of the Ming dynasty against the invading Manchus who founded the new Ching dynasty in 1644. But gradually the Manchus established themselves and produced great emperors, and the secret societies drifted into crime and began running the big protection rackets in Chinese cities. They were tightly organized and powerful. The father of the Chinese Republic, Sun Yat Sen was glad of their help in recruiting support. From early days they were active in Hong Kong.

"But that's all over now," police spokesmen were saying back in the 1960s. " The Triads aren't the big organizations they used to be, with all their abracadabra of initiation ceremonies, tattooing and oaths of brotherhood. There is no central direction. They are just small fragmented gangs, the sort of nuisance you get in any big city. We are gradually eliminating them, and we could move faster if their victims — members of the public — would only come forward with information and complaints."

In the last thirty years the Triads have not only not disappeared, they have penetrated deeper into local life.

A large new restaurant in one of the New Towns paid the sum of Hong Kong $8,888 on its opening day (For the Chinese, eight is an auspicious number); and five thousand dollars monthly for continuing "protection".

"Everyone pays up," the proprietor told a close friend. "If you fail to do so, or make a report to the police, the Brothers simply come into your place and cause trouble and disturbance, so the genuine customers leave. You go broke in no time." The owner of a smaller restaurant in the Causeway Bay area admitted to paying two thousand dollars a month and said this was normal.

If shops, restaurants and cinemas are all paying up, this represents a turnover of uncountable millions. And this is an industry employing thousands of strong-arm operators, many of them working only part-time when called upon; and of course it pays no business tax.

Schoolchildren are now included in the secret society activities.

"I wouldn't let my kids play down in the basket ball ground," says a mother in a housing estate. "That's where the Black Society does its recruiting. The same goes for pinball parlours."

Why does Hong Kong provide such fertile ground for the Triad societies to operate? The answer lies partly in the ancient Chinese tradition of men of

spirit and integrity helping each other survive in a hostile and corrupt society. It's a Robin Hood theme immortalized in the Chinese classic *The Water Margin*, calculated to appeal to the young and restless. The school world of Hong Kong is ruthlessly academic, with much emphasis on cramming for examinations; if you don't have a specially good memory, if you're clever with your hands but can't retain thousands of Chinese characters in your head, you lose out badly. And the Brothers are waiting round the corner to tell you how to enjoy the big time by being smart and taking the short cuts.

Success in recruiting among the young people ensures the secret societies' survival and growth. If villains approach you with demands for protection money, simply report to us, say the police. Yes, but how can you be sure that your report won't be leaked by some Mafia character who's wormed his way into the Force, and a night or two later, when you're homeward bound on a dark night — no, better not risk it. Leave it to the police to do their own campaigning, their own infiltration of the Black Society.

Teenage Triads have long been operating in some Hong Kong schools. They've concentrated on extorting fellow pupils' pocket money, bullying, providing schoolgirls with prostitution money by introducing them to businessmen. The girl receives five hundred dollars for an afternoon, keeps two hundred for herself, hands the rest over to Triad liaison.

Some Hong Kong businesses are especially vulnerable to Triad pressures. Interior decoration is one. When government flats are allotted it's left to the new tenant to arrange his own plastering and finishing. He will soon be advised by a "friend" to choose one particular company, whose strong-arm operatives will wreck the place if they are denied the contract. "But you're talking about the past," said a police spokesman back in 1974. " That no longer happens."

If it stopped, it has certainly started again. It came as an even bigger shock to the general public to learn that the Triads were also into property speculation. Property companies like to encourage an atmosphere of feverish demand — pictures of anxious flat-buyers queuing through the night to snap up what's going. Triad men were soon muscling in, pushing people out of their places, taking over the head of the queue and defying anyone to protest. On one notorious occasion a large Triad group so massively interfered with the presale of flats at Cheung Kong's Laguna City development last year that the police were called in and warned them off.

The incident showed how gang leaders can mobilize a sizable force when needed. Their supporters will not be full-time gangsters but men pursuing normal occupations who can be called on as required.

More recently the Hong Kong film industry — one of the biggest in the Far East — has been calling for police protection. Directors, actors and actresses have been alleging openly that they were threatened with violence unless they agreed to take part in certain films the Triads were financing. Not all the victims have clear consciences themselves. They may be members of rival Triads and their film companies may be under the protection of Triad competition.

A cinema owner complained he was being ruined by demands by Black Society groups for thousands of free tickets.

As for the more usual protection rackets, these have been part of Hong Kong life since anyone can remember. Illegal gambling clubs, dance halls, brothels, shopkeepers, hawkers — they are all the prey of the Black Society.

The Triads are also into loan-sharking. The various societies share out the gambling territory in Macau. As the Hong Kong working man emergences from the Lisboa Hotel there, gloomily brooding on the loss of everything he's earned in a month, they are waiting in the dark street. Of course they are ready to see him through his immediate money problems, but the interest they charge will make it certain he'll never be free of their clutches. They'll imprison him in a hotel room until he can raise the money under threats of violence. He's under no legal obligation to meet their astronomical demands but fear makes him pay up.

How does the average Hong Kong citizen react to Triad activity in local life? "My father was approached for money," says a technician's daughter, "and it was a very worrying situation. But he went and saw a man he knew who had connections with the Triads. I don't know who he was, only that he had some tie-up. And we weren't bothered any more."

A young housing estate dweller told how family life was made unbearable

All these discreet enterprises—the acupressure parlours, short-stay small hotels, brothels, gambling—pay the Triads. And so does legitimate business.

by the noisy Triad parties going on in the flat below. His father went down to complain and was threatened with violence. There was a fight and his father was told the "Brothers would come and settle his affair." "They cut our washing lines and burned lots of paper outside our door to smoke us out and make life as miserable as possible. But my father knew someone with the right connections and he went and talked to this man, who contacted the Triads and they worked out a settlement. We wanted our father to go to the police but he preferred the indirect approach. Actually our go-between was in the C.I.D."

It's difficult to know accurately how far the Black Society's influence stretches because people prefer not to talk about it. Rumours abound of Triad operators making huge fortunes in the upper echelons of business, carrying on their dirty work behind the facade of a respected name. "Wherever there's big money the Triads are sure to be muscling in," says a local lawyer, "but every level of society is affected, if only indirectly. Your lowly employee will not be troubled, but the boss may be paying up. A professional man, a doctor will receive a polite note through the letter box saying the Brothers are meeting problems and will he please leave ten thousand in cash in a cigarette tin behind the staircase on the sixth floor of a certain neighbouring block?

"The doctor will almost certainly comply. Go to the police and you may run into a lot of bother and red tape. Better pay up and hope that's the end of it."

"You are on your way to work and someone taps you on the shoulder and says quietly that the Brothers expect a small contribution from you — say a hundred. And you quickly hand it over because it's easier that way." Interviewed for a TV documentary on street markets, a legal hawker says of course payments have to be made but he would prefer not to discuss it.

The police are always asking for information from victims so the villains can be prosecuted. It's a crime in Hong Kong even to belong to a Triad society. Loan-sharks lending money above a certain rate of interest are sent to prison and the borrower is under no compulsion to pay. Yet the Triads survive and flourish. It's something in the temperament of the Southern Chinese, as in that of the Sicilians and Southern Italians, that seems to tolerate this kind of black organization.

What about the China Mainland? After the Communists came to power in 1949, secret societies were eliminated; but now there is growing evidence of their revival. A Communist Party spokesman was even quoted not long ago as saying that Triad societies were not so evil if they were truly patriotic — a statement found most discouraging by social reformers in Hong Kong.

Triads are also known to be active among overseas Chinese communities — in Taiwan, Britain, the United States. It's believed that, with the uncertainties hanging over Hong Kong daily life after 1997, Triad organizations have been transferring some of their assets and regular rackets to areas abroad where the police are less experienced in dealing with their traditional methods. Cases involving Triad-related murders have already come to light in London and New York in the past few years.

Chapter 13

Education Is the Key

"One thing I am absolutely determined about," said the young secretary returning from her honeymoon. "My children are going to university, no matter what!"

This intelligent Chinese girl, child of poor parents, had worked hard at school and stayed on until she was eighteen; but university was beyond her reach. Homework for advanced and complicated subjects was anyway difficult in a 600 square foot flat crowded with other family members and in her days only one out of three students who qualified expected a university place in Hong Kong. So she took a clerical job in a big Western conglomerate, and filled her evenings with extramural studies in management, German and computers.

It's an ancient tradition among the Chinese that formal education is vital to success in life. Up to modern

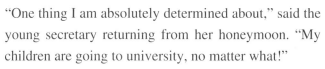

If you want your child to succeed, start with the right kindergarten. The Western ones go in for "learning through play", but in the traditional establishments they start with Chinese characters from the word go.

times it was always the scholars, the men who passed the state examinations, who did the governing, and the ignorant, the masses, who had to do as they were told.

A university degree counts for far more in Asia than in the West. It commands a reasonable starting salary. It installs you decisively on the right side of the ravine separating those who get their hands dirty from the ones who sit behind the big desks.

How does that principle work out in Hong Kong? Pragmatic views prevail, the aim being a job which pays well and facilitates emigration.

And, there are now about three times as many higher education places here as there were fifteen years ago — including two polytechnics and a new technical university, the Baptist College and Lingnan.

The University of Hong Kong is no longer the magnet it used to be, simply because there are so many more institutions of higher learning now, and undergraduates are less interested in arts subjects and instead go for scientific and technical courses. If you study literature, where can that take you? Nobody in the Chinese world, with the exception of the kung-fu-writing editor of the *Ming Pao Daily News*, Mr. Louis Cha, has ever made a living from writing. Journalism in Hong Kong is shockingly paid; if you support a family, you will be working for three newspapers at once. Few students want to take medicine nowadays, this in striking contrast with previous years. "Of course a doctor is well paid," said a school-leaver, "but it takes five years of study followed by a tough year as houseman in a government hospital. Whereas computers or engineering means you're certain of a good job after only three years' training, with no problems over emigrating. You can't practise as a doctor in Britain or Canada on the strength of Hong Kong qualifications (though a Hong Kong-trained pharmacist can enter Canada)."

At all costs, go for the white-collar jobs.

"I was taken aback," said a Western director. "We had this messenger boy who was really bright, so we thought we would groom him for a top position, take him right through the firm's processes, starting with various factory jobs and then introduce him to management and send him on courses. But his widowed mother was dead against it, wouldn't see reason. She wanted him

The new Hong Kong University of Science and Technology attracts many students, convinced that a course in computing brings more solid, quicker returns than medicine or the arts.

kept in the office in a white-collar job, away from all that dirty machinery and noise. So we had to give up our plan. And that was a pity. A man who's been through the hoop, knows all the departments, is worth so much more to us than some ignorant young university graduate who expects to start as an assistant manager."

The lives of conscientious Hong Kong parents are haunted by education. First you need a good kindergarten that will help the child into a good school. And a kindergarten is not just a place for playing around with other children. You start writing and learning Chinese characters and pass tests which will earn you a kindergarten diploma; and this means you'll steal a march on your competitors and be able to enter one of the good schools. A good school, in local parlance, doesn't usually mean a government school, but rather one of the well-known establishments founded long ago by foreign missionary organizations. Places in these schools are anxiously competed for, though now a certain number of less-gifted pupils have to be admitted by government directive.

You hear a group of wealthy well-dressed wives at a formal party talking passionately together. What about? A marital scandal or an expected run on some husband's bank? Not at all. They're bewailing the difficulty of getting young Marmaduke or Mei-ling into that much desired school — how tough the nuns were against admitting them, even though the grandmother had been a pupil and the children had graduated with honours from kindergarten.

The foreigner may wonder why Chinese children often have Western

Small Chinese children enjoy dressing up and performing to the delight of speech day audiences.

names as well as the Chinese names given them by parents. The answer is that in many schools Western teachers find it difficult to memorize Chinese names so the children are given Western names for convenience's sake. "During my school years we were studying Dickens' *David Copperfield*. You remember the girl David marries is called Agnes? That was the name the teacher gave me."

The standards in most Hong Kong schools, from a Western point of view, are very demanding and extremely academic. Students are expected to absorb knowledge like human sponges. The best schools are enlightened, urging students to think of the world outside and their places in it. Student councils and clubs organize such out-of-school activities as social service to old people and the mentally handicapped. More time is spent on sport than formerly. Yet the scene is still, by Western standards, old-fashioned. The children are in school to work and learn, not question or criticize or spend afternoons in games.

"Our son was getting ninety-six and ninety-eight per cent in his tests," said a worried parent, "and then he dropped to ninety. We were called in by his teacher to know why he was slipping. Were we supervising his homework closely enough? The boy couldn't sleep, started having nightmares." Parents will call in private tutors for holiday work. For older students tutoring is a way of earning pocket money during the holidays. Overconscientious mothers sit by their children overlooking their homework, making sure they've written everything out correctly. Knuckle-rapping and use of a short cane are not at all unknown; it's all for the child's good.

The teacher has traditionally been revered among the Chinese. He's been seen as a dedicated figure solely concerned with the well-being and intellectual progress of his students — always miserably paid but widely respected.

A Chinese man from Beijing recalled his former teacher as a man who admitted that in twenty-two years he could never afford a new suit. He would come to school always in the same shabby jacket which he would transfer to a metal hanger during lessons, wearing instead an even shabbier garment for working hours. But he commanded enormous authority.

Until recently you would never hear, in Hong Kong, of a teacher being "ragged" by unruly teenagers, or having to resign because of failure to keep order.

However respect for teachers has diminished here. Many of them are dedicated but many — including those in government employ — carry out their relatively well-paid work with no special enthusiasm.

Changing education policies have confronted them with new problems. Since nine years schooling (six to fifteen) became compulsory, many unwilling teenagers are still in school though they can't keep up with the demanding academic standards. This means a harder time for the teacher and frustration all round. It's an ironic situation. Schools which once could pick and choose new students are now obliged to take more of a cross-section. In some cases this may mean unruly or bored youngsters negating the teacher's efforts, but they can't be expelled because education is compulsory.

It's a scene of contrasts. At the top the prestige schools where pupils work hard, supervised by parents expecting great results; and at the other end of the spectrum the schools of lesser quality, attended by children whose parents are both working long hours to keep the home going and haven't time to be interested in the children's schoolwork. What they do know is that although education is free up to the age of fifteen, there are bus fares, lunch money and textbooks to pay for, costing hundreds of dollars a month.

There have always been men who felt strongly that they would succeed despite their inability to master Chinese literature, philosophy, science and mathematics. Hong Kong tycoons have risen from the ranks of salesmen and small property developers; the stock exchange has produced big-time gamblers who've coined millions while their hunches lasted.

"It's true I left school early. My family needed the money. We were living in an old flat, sleeping five to a room, and I worked my way up through experience on the building sites," says a local foreman. "So did other men I could mention. Look at Li Ka Shing. He never went to college. Old people in Wanchai remember him going round selling plastic material. It seems he was a very polite salesman."

A relatively new experiment in Hong Kong is that of the prevocational schools which cater for the less academically gifted and train them in specialized crafts while also providing a normal education. Some have proved a success but parents have been begging the education authorities for a more academic curriculum.

In Hong Kong now a new generation is invading the scene with attitudes unknown to their parents. They leave school early, as soon as they're fifteen, get holiday jobs in fast-food places or as messengers in firms and earn three or four thousand a month. They go around in groups haunting the *karaokes* and discos, the pinball parlours and, rucksacks on backs, set off on expeditions to the islands for barbecues and picnics.

Respect for teachers and education is one of the yardsticks by which Hong Kong people judge the Communist Mainland.

Mao Zedong was himself a conscientious student. His ethics teacher at Changsha Normal School gave him full marks for his essays. Mao married his

A school wins prestige with successes on sports day. Promising athletes are given special training, but the rest tend to lose out.

daughter. However the nearest Mao came to university life was his job as assistant librarian at Beijing University. He believed that practical experience was the best teacher. Later he would write of tertiary education: "One or two years at university may be useful for a few students who will afterwards return to productive labour." He confessed to ignorance of economics and he thought abstract research a waste of time. The only research of any value, he insisted, was that closely related to current production.

An early campaign promised by the Communists was universal education. It was to prove an embarrassment for the Party leaders when the higher academic levels were often reached by the children of "political reactionaries." There were books and a general feeling for literacy in some of these homes of former officials and capitalists. Inevitably their offsprings performed better than the children of peasants and soldiers. When the politically unreliable were excluded and replaced by the politically sound, university academic standards were bound to suffer.

The most crippling blows to education on the Mainland were dealt in the Cultural Revolution, when teenagers were encouraged to shout down and physically attack their teachers. "You can argue that Chinese education systems need an overhaul to meet the needs of the modern world," said an overseas Chinese intellectual, "but that's the last thing the Cultural Revolution was ever likely to achieve." During those fateful years the universities and many middle schools were shut down. The results are to be seen among many of today's Mainland professionals; it's the young who are the liveliest in grasping new ideas, new technology. The middle-aged often lack both know-how and initiative. They came to manhood in the lost years.

The present situation on the Mainland, according to Beijing's own statistics, is that even primary education is unavailable in a quarter of the rural counties. Middle schools are practically non-existent in the countryside but are organized in "most of the cities." As for universities, only two per cent of young men and women in their late teens and early twenties are actually in college, compared with close on fifty per cent in the United States. Beijing spoke recently of a "serious lack of science and economic graduates" — the human force needed to advance China's industry in today's world.

It might be thought that these problems hardly concern the vast army of China's peasants, absorbed in the day-to-day necessities of growing enough food and surviving floods, droughts and typhoons. However life in China is changing not only in the cities but also in the villages. The farmers and local officials, having abandoned the commune system, are working together to set up local factories producing farm tools, cement, clothing, electrical appliances. The need is growing for educated managers and skilled foremen. All China, it might seem, is crying out for better education. Especially in the cities the restlessness of youth is expressed in a growing interest in learning Western languages — mainly English — as a means to study in a foreign university or polytechnic and the chance of a permanent job abroad.

All this is well-known to parents and teachers in Hong Kong, keenly aware of 1997. Nowadays fewer graduates here are entering the teaching profession, and more teachers are changing to other jobs more likely to score points with Australian, Canadian and American immigration authorities.

Last year pre-migration counselling was revived by the Hong Kong branch of International Social Service. The seminars and interviews were nearly all attended by families with children. All would rather stay in Hong Kong than emigrate, but what kind of education can children expect in Hong Kong after 1997? This is the main cause of anxiety in the minds of parents. And if they emigrate, what are likely to be the difficulties for a Hong Kong educated child adapting to life in Australia or North America?

Some families have spent the requisite three years in Canada, applied for and received naturalization and then returned to Hong Kong. Some are determined to stay here, knowing they have the means to escape if the local scene clouds over. Others are continuing a new life abroad and won't return — because of the children.

One mother said, " The North American system of education was an eye-opener to us. The children are actually encouraged to think for themselves, to question received wisdom and show initiative. It means that as teenagers they are often barely sufferable, but they do have a chance to grow up into self-reliant men and women, unafraid of authority and ready to speak out. Here the children have to swot and worry too much."

In the primary schools and even in kindergartens Hong Kong children are introduced to computers.

Some children can't take it. Several times during the school year the newspapers will carry the report of a suicide — some adolescent unable to bear the shame of being punished for a misdemeanour, or of failing an examination and not daring to face parental anger. "The sight which upsets me," said an American parent, "is that of a Hong Kong pupil of three years old — yes, three! — in tears because of trouble over homework! That is ridiculous by any standards."

Education in Hong Kong, for nearly all Chinese, means mastering the thousands of characters of the Chinese language, and the Chinese style of writing. From any junior schoolroom, hour after hour, emerges the rhythmic noise of young voices chanting, chanting, committing phrases to memory. A boy or girl of fourteen should know enough to read a newspaper. For those who find such serious reading too heavy a burden there's a large-scale industry developed for producing books of cartoons with minimal texts, or an easy-to-read teenage-oriented magazine like *Yes!* which publishes advice on dating the opposite sex, and runs a competition for deciding the ugliest school uniform (which upset local school principals). In later teenage the student will know enough to tackle novels and political magazines although for a classic like *Dream of the Red Chamber* with its poetic quotations and descriptions of dresses and interiors they'll still have to consult the dictionary at times.

"We had a special day at our school," said a young friend of my wife, "to make us all keener on writing well in Chinese; and we wrote big-character posters to advertise it and stuck them up near the Star Ferry. And an old Chinese man passing by looked at our posters and said: "Judging by those characters you certainly do need to do something about your Chinese pretty urgently."

It was a Chinese friend who declared to us, when we first arrived in Hong Kong, that the public signs here are written in the most appalling Chinese. He said they were usually drawn up by expatriate officials; and their Chinese assistants, wishing to make the boss happy, insisted that the phrasing was perfectly elegant and could not have been done better.

Most schools in Hong Kong teach in both English and Chinese. English is supposed to be the main medium of instruction (except for such subjects as Chinese literature and history and Chinese language) but most teachers feel happier teaching their students in Chinese and so, although they use textbooks printed in English the spoken language in the classroom is mostly Chinese. The trouble with this "mixed code" pattern of teaching and learning is that standards are slipping in both Chinese and English. The Education Department is still battling with this problem.

The best end-products of Hong Kong education, the youngsters from prestigious schools who have passed all their tests and won honours at university, are very impressive human beings. The Chinese are particularly outstanding in mathematics and science. They ought to be used far more than at present in technological research to keep Hong Kong in the forefront of Far East development. As it is many business observers say the territory is slipping behind other more far-sighted industrial competitors such as South Korea and Singapore.

Chapter 14

Festivals

It's often said the Chinese are not a religious people, but that is an over-simplification. There are half a million Chinese Christians in Hong Kong as well as large numbers of Buddhists, Taoists and Muslims and followers of Hinduism.

Generally speaking, however, the Chinese are not given to mysticism — a deep concern with their relationship to an Unseen Power. The ancestors may be watching what you do, but God is not worrying over the state of your soul. Hong Kong Chinese Christians are loyal to their

Getting ready for the Bun Festival on Cheung Chau island.

churches and regular in attending services; but their approach to life is practical.

In many Chinese households here, it is true, you will find a shrine dedicated to the land god but this is usually looked after by the mother of the family, who provides offerings of chicken, wine, tea and pork on the first and fifteenth days of the lunar month. It would be the depth of bad behaviour to treat the shrine with disrespect. Yet after a modern young couple get married and settle into their own flat, what then? "We bring out the shrine when Mother calls, but after she's gone we shove it back under the bed," said a wife in her twenties.

The scene is changing all the time. In a restless place like Hong Kong attitudes and behaviour adapt year after year to the pressures of business and social life. Chinese who lack fervent belief still find satisfaction and pleasure in the observance of festivals and ceremonies. This is an exotic aspect of the ways of the Chinese, setting them apart from others and establishing a special rhythm in their lives.

Origins of festivals are lost in the mists of time. At first they may have been held to propitiate spirits of earth, sea, rivers and storms — the forces that decide whether you starve or survive. But the Chinese like to humanize things, and invented stories of immortals and humans have breathed life into thousand-year-old rites and made them familiar.

Festivals vary enormously in popularity. Some, like the Bun Festival on Cheung Chau island and the Dragon Boat races, attract the tourists. Others are very much family affairs. You hardly expect foreign acquaintance to show up when you sweep the graves at Ching Ming. That means "Clear and Bright" and the festival reminds the Westerner of Easter, for it marks the overtaking of winter by returning spring. For Chinese it's the occasion to show respect for the ancestors. You bow three times to their graves, offer the quantities of food brought for the occasion, and with all rites duly performed, the food (as the spirits don't touch it) can be taken home and eaten. The other festival emphasizing respect for forbears is Chung Yeung (held on the ninth day of the ninth moon). According to legend a man named Huan Ching was warned by his teacher on this day to take his family to high ground at all costs. He did so and on returning next day found his livestock and pets had perished instead of

On Ching Ming Festival, falling at roughly the same time of year as Easter, families sweep the graves of ancestors and make traditional offerings.

himself and family. Ever afterwards on this day families visit high ground and, as many graves are on the hill-slopes, take the opportunity of paying respects to ancestors. Nowadays certain customs meticulously observed by parents are not always followed by children and grandchildren. Westerners reading up volumes on Chinese traditions will be surprised to find a Chinese friend almost unaware of the Festival of Flowers, or the Festival of Lanterns that follows Lunar New Year.

Chinese New Year, the great holiday, is a largely family affair. It is a good idea for Westerners to call on Chinese friends at this festival season

The character on the red *lai see* packets means "blessing".

but they must make sure to do it on the right day — not the third day of the festival which is fraught with the prospect of quarrelling after so much eating and celebration. Cantonese and Northern conventions tend to differ. Some Cantonese will tell you it brings bad luck to call after dark; others say they've heard of no such thing. In any case it is better not to hang around if you break in on a mah-jong party. If you are married red envelopes containing money in duplicated amounts — two fives, two tens, or two hundreds, should be given to children, unmarried young ladies and servants. In Hong Kong it is usual to have the actual name-character of the donor on the envelopes. The most common family names are already printed on red envelopes you can buy in the shops.

For many people in Hong Kong and on the Mainland (though there they call it the Spring Festival) Lunar New Year means more than any other festival. All-night flower markets draw the crowds before the first day; extra trains carry thousand upon thousand of passengers to spend the festival with relatives in Mainland towns and villages. In Hong Kong life virtually stops, most of the shops are shut — and even the restaurants, for cooks and waiters are also at home celebrating.

Never mind what days are marked in official calendars, factory and construction workers usually take a whole week off at New Year. And unlike the Western world, here the big shops hold their sales before the holidays, not after. This helps keep up the old tradition that everyone should have new clothes before the New Year. They must also visit the hairdresser, who of course doubles the prices to celebrate the festival.

According to tradition all debts must be repaid before Lunar New Year. Even the underworld respects this time-honoured tradition and that's said

Peach trees and oranges on sale in Victoria Park on the night before Lunar New Year.

Tin Hau Festival at Yuen Long village. The Goddess on her shrine ceremonially paraded.

to be the reason for the spate of burglaries and pickpocketing just before New Year starts. However the world of honest business is changing, as a Hong Kong merchant explained. This is an era of contracts and loans with varying expiry dates, and so the old rigid settling of accounts by Old Year's night is a smaller factor in local life.

The Goddess of the Sea, Tien Hou, still commands her following among the fishing folk and other seagoing people; hers is the most colourful and lively of the year's festivals. On her day, the 23rd of the Third Moon, all the junks are dressed with flags and make their way to various shrines on islands and promontories dedicated to this young girl who saved the lives of seamen from shipwreck, centuries ago. For a Westerner it's a wonderful way of passing a lively day on the water, although you need some contact with a boat-people family to get a ride. There's a deal of drumming and lion dancing, and a curious procedure at the temples, where young men fight to secure

The Dragon Boat Festival races enlivened Hong Kong life long before the high-rise housing estates changed the sky-line.

lucky numbers fired from bamboo cannons.

Forty years ago a keen student of Chinese customs, Valentine Burckhardt wrote that "there is something extremely friendly about a Chinese religious festival. All classes attend but there is not the slightest distinction among them apart from dress. Ladies in silks sit next to boat people in their customary black, or amahs, hawkers or shopgirls, conversing as if they had known one another all their lives. It must be remembered that there is no weekly Sunday break for the Chinese and that the pilgrimages (like the mediaeval festivals in Europe described in *The Canterbury Tales*) correspond to the modern Bank Holiday ..."

How times change! Ladies in silk sitting in junks talking like old friends with hawkers and amahs? Gone with the wind. Hong Kong has thrown up a great bourgeois middle class since those mediaeval days and affluence has so often meant a loss of the common touch.

It's only in recent years that the Dragon Boat Festival has been developed into an international tourist attraction through the publicity work of the Hong Kong Tourist Association. The long thin craft racing through the spray are an extraordinary sight. Expatriates from far and wide as well as local associations enter teams and compete for trophies. Women's teams have acquitted themselves impressively.

The origin of the festival was probably some rite of propitiation, to persuade the river god not to flood the fields; but the human legend tells of the minister-poet Chu Yuan who drowned himself in the Mi Lo River in Hunan province in protest against a corrupt government. Boats raced in a vain attempt to save him. Specially-made rice-dumplings were thrown in the water to feed the fish and stop them eating Chu Yuan. Nowadays people eat the dumplings themselves to commemorate him.

Festival stories survive in varying versions; one of the most endearing illustrates the Seventh Sister, honoured on the seventh day of the seventh moon. She was the daughter of the Kitchen God in Heaven but she came down to earth and fell in love with a handsome cowherd, and married him. Her father sent heavenly messengers and took her back after a struggle, but, in answer to her tearful pleadings, allowed the couple to spend just one night together every year, and the stars were consolidated into the Milky Way to form a bridge by which they could meet. Another version says the bridge was formed not by stars but by magpies.

Anyway the Seventh of the Seventh is especially a festival for young women seeking husbands, and for amahs.

The Westerner is puzzled by so many references to the lunar calendar. Why are so many Chinese festivals depending on the moon? "But aren't many of your Christian festivals based on the moon rather than the Gregorian calendar?" asks your Chinese friend. "And besides, there is a traditional faith among us that the lunar calendar is more reliable. For instance at Ching Ming it always rains. At Chung Yeung it is always sunny; at the time of the Dragon Boat Festival you have showers but not enough to spoil the proceedings. The day of the Winter Solstice is very cold; and the Mid-Autumn Festival always brings good weather so you can enjoy the sight of the Moon."

"Are you serious? You mean the lunar calendar is as reliable as all that?"

"Well, yes, more or less. That's the general belief."

Simple people keep old ways alive. It's in the back streets, in the hot August season, that they burn so much paper along the gutters. This is the season of the Hungry Ghosts, a great festival celebrated especially among the Teochew people, who come from

Lanterns for sale at Mid-Autumn Festival in many shapes and sizes: rabbits, fishes and even cars, and planes.

an area of five countries in the east of Guangdong province and have settled in great numbers in Hong Kong.

Why are the ghosts hungry? The official title is simply Festival of the Ghosts, dating from the time of Emperor Wu of the Liang dynasty (502–507). He had a dream in which he was told to organize prayers for the veneration of the dead. He subsequently had an altar built on the Gold Mountain as a centre for the ceremonies. Celebration of the festival includes making donations to Buddhist priests as a way of expressing gratitude to parents, ancestors and the world of spirits. But many people see in the festival a way of propitiating, with food offerings, the ghosts of those who have died without funeral rites — in war or by drowning at sea.

In Hong Kong the Ghosts celebrations include a great deal of charitable giving, not only to Taoist and Buddhist priests, but also to the hungry and dispossessed. Chinese operas and puppet shows draw big crowds. Legend has it that once, when a man named Mu Nien was offering his dead mother a bowl of cooked rice he became aware that she was surrounded by hungry ghosts. The rice burst into flames in her mouth. In his distress he appealed to Buddha, who explained that the mother's sins were so great that her son must seek the help of all the gods and senior Buddhist priests, and prepare delicacies and fruits as sacrifices. By carrying out these instructions Mu Nien was able to rescue his mother from hell.

It is believed in Hong Kong that a great part of the expenses of the Hungry

Ghosts Festival and ceremonies associated with it is borne by underworld figures, as a means of making amends to the gods for the crimes they've committed during the rest of the year.

All the paper objects burning in the side-streets are for the comfort of the dead in their own ghostly world — furniture, clothes, telephones, TV sets — even credit cards!

Autumn brings the harvest moon, when people go to high places to take a close look at the moon in its glory while children play with brightly-lit lanterns in the shapes of birds, fruits and animals. Savoury moon cakes are given to relatives and friends and some Western palates may find them an acquired taste. For when it comes to sweet and savoury things, Chinese and Western palates may react quite differently.

"Of course I'll be eating dinner at home tonight," said a Chinese friend. "It is the Winter Solstice — that's more important than Chinese New Year."

This is the quietest festival of the whole calendar because then almost everybody eats at home. An outsider can live here for years without knowing anything about it. Yet its origins go deep — this idea of families coming together on the longest night of the year, in the depth of winter, to take comfort in the certainty that from now on the days will grow longer and the earth will awake and be warm again.

Festivals are vital to the psychological health of a Chinese. They chart the year, they are signposts and milestones. They cause a man to think of his ancestors and of those who will come after, of the long continuous history of his race.

For the Westerner the strangest Chinese festivals of all are the *Ta Tsui* rites, held in certain villages in the New Territories every ten years. In many places they've been abandoned as the villages were swallowed up by the bricks and mortar of the expanding city, but where they survive they are very grand affairs, with images of the gods brought in from miles around, great mat-sheds put up for the ceremonies and entertainment, hiring of priests, summoning of all villagers from near and far.

Former inhabitants even come back from Australia and America, driving out to the village in big cars, wealthy families who've made the big time but

The King of the Ghosts towers above the watching mortals. At nightfall they will burn him, but he'll reappear next year.

never forget their origins. When the week of celebration is over and they've all gone again, then the village sinks back into its rustic daily life. A whole world is gradually dying, ancestral halls decaying, young men leaving for foreign places — but the festivals add joyful noise, colour and ritual to the sunset glow.

The aim of most village ceremonies and festivals has always been protection. The visitor strolling among the picturesque houses has no idea of the harshness of life in days still remembered. Unseen Forces might bring disease to the children, death among the cattle. Propitiation was all-important — you begged the gods to be kind, you celebrated and praised them in the hope of being spared.

The small farmer lives at the mercy of the weather, prices fluctuating in faraway markets, competition from across the border and the whims of a hundred deities. Compared to this even the toughest factory job, because of regular wages and time off, means easy living.

Chapter 15

Opera and Cantonese Magic — The Great Revival

They queue all day for tickets; so many want to book at once that the Urbtix computer breaks down under the pressure. The theatres are packed and at the end of a performance lasting nearly four hours the young people surge to the front of the auditorium, applauding, taking pictures. And then round to the stage door, to await impatiently the moment for presenting the emerging stars with flowers and soft toys. This is Cantonese opera, the great local element in today's Hong Kong scene.

It's become especially popular in the last ten years. They even include excerpts in the discs cut for *karaoke*, that new singing craze that's taken the Asian world by storm. Classes in Cantonese operatic singing and stage training have multiplied. Books about it are published in Chinese and English and seminars discuss the opera's

In *The Royal Beauty* the young man declares his love against the background of the statue of Guan Yin — Goddess of Mercy.

derivation and influence. There are Cantonese opera courses and clubs in the universities.

It flourishes despite the cinema, television, disco. It expresses the essential culture of the Cantonese — their feelings towards life, love and fate. And the talent, the enthusiasm and the big audiences are all here in Hong Kong, rather than across the border in Guangdong. Back in the 1950s and early 1960s black-and-white filmed versions of Cantonese opera made up forty per cent of all showings at Chinese cinemas in Hong Kong. Then it was in decline for a while. All an outsider might know about it was the enormous network of scaffolding going up at some village like Shek O, a mat-shed temporary theatre with places for several thousand — existing just for the week, in celebration of such local deities as Tian Hou, who cares for those who seek their living on the sea.

Village people take these festive performances very seriously. For them there's a religious meaning unknown to the city people and foreign visitors.

They'll stage a scene-setter for the gods, its origin lost in the mists of time.

A Western newcomer taken to a Cantonese opera performance is likely to be the only non-Chinese in the theatre. A strange experience, that first visit. What is it all about, why all this enthusiasm? What horrible noises the orchestra makes, do they call this music? And the snarling, whining and chanting of the actors — what on earth has this to do with real life or a truly creative art form? Not only Westerners but also many Hong Kong Chinese reject it as the noisy and boring entertainment of an older, more limited generation.

The fact is, Chinese opera is a very Chinese affair with its own standards of excellence, and you acquire a taste for it gradually. It takes time to appreciate the techniques, enriched by all the accumulated skills and experience of thousands of actors and actresses down the centuries. And it's only when you know more about the symbols and conventions that you, the outsider, begin to enjoy the show as Chinese enthusiasts do.

Almost every region of China has its own version and style of opera and most critics have held that Peking opera is the highest form. But many Hong Kong people disagree. They don't follow northern speech so easily and Cantonese opera is closer to them, more deeply rooted in the local soil. They

Cantonese operatic singing was staged at the Tin Hau Festival in this temporary theatre on Cheung Chau island.

enjoy the range of its morality-play characters — villains, heroes, princesses, soldiers, merchants, sweethearts and lovers — a change from the daily environment of Hong Kong. With some it's part of a growing interest in the Chinese history and legends the operas illustrate; with others it's a search, through the operas, for something missing from their daily lives — ideal love, a handsome and well-educated husband, a clear black-and-white distinction between good and evil.

There's plenty of choice of theme — about eleven thousand Cantonese operas have been written in the last seven centuries or so. As the name "opera" implies there's a great deal of singing and, as in all forms of Chinese opera, conventional, highly elaborate make-up identifies the characters as soon as they appear — the scarlet-painted face denotes loyalty and uprightness; white paint for the bad men; and pennants and eight-foot pheasant feathers for military commanders. There's not much development of character but the nuances of temperament, age and emotion are conveyed by talents born of endless training and rehearsal. Versatility is transsexual — women playing men's parts and vice versa. And you may see an actress in her mid-twenties in the role of a grandmother conveying every slight osteoporosis stiffness of the hip, every weariness of the raised arm; and a mature woman star movingly representing the young man in love.

It's the most severely stylized form of theatre in the world, surely, all this posturing and declaiming of emperors, princes and generals, mincing gestures of concubines gorgeous as tropical butterflies with make-up and costume rigidly decided to indicate rank and character. You have to know the conventions of stage management; the carrying of a fringed whip to show the actor's on horseback; a chair symbolizing a prison with the actor kneeling behind a chair peering through the back supports as if through barred windows. But nowadays naturalism is growing; the scenery — one large backdrop — reaches to the top of the stage.

Why the new and growing popularity of Cantonese opera among students and intellectuals? Hard to say. It seems only yesterday that the educated, condescending view was that this was just a form of mass entertainment for the servants and factory hands. Yet, after a decade or two of decline it quickly caught on again , and now there are more up-and-coming, bright young people taking part in productions.

A Hong Kong government servant said: "The scores and libretti are outstanding. The lowlier characters speak in a common tongue; the noble rhetoric is for the high-ups. It's the libretti which attract me most. And the acting in the lead roles is superb."

He was talking about the most popular Cantonese opera troupe performing in Hong Kong at that time — the Chor Fung Ming, the offshoot of an older, highly respected group. Chor Fung Ming means something like "singing of the young phoenix." In 1990 it dominated the local opera scene and was responsible for some 125 out of the 1,000 or so operatic performances given in Hong Kong, and its repertoire of more than thirty operas includes many of the works of the legendary Tang Di-sheng. Tang, a famous playwright of the 1950s and 1960s, wrote libretti of a quality to arouse interest and enthusiasm among the young and educated.

In the opera *The Royal Beauty* the heroine disguised as a Taoist nun at the fall of the Ming dynasty is discovered by her long lost husband. The couple are the two principal actors of the Chor Fung Ming Cantonese Opera Troupe.

Playing the most important male parts was the actress Long Kim-sang; and the female leads were taken by her woman colleague Mei Suet-shi. Both studied under famous operatic performers, Ren Kim-fai (she also played male roles) and Bai Suet-xian. The influence of these teachers has been very powerful; the operas they produced often figure prominently in today's opera repertoires, although the Chor Fung Ming has been disbanded (Long Kim-sang went to Canada). They are repeated again and again but the audiences never seem to tire. They pack the theatres.

In 1990 Long received the Artist of the Year Award for stage performance. She said at the time that her success was due to the tough and serious training she had received from her two teachers, one of whom, Bai, is still alive. Ren died in 1989 and huge crowds of opera-lovers were at the funeral. Critics feel Long has inherited many of her qualities. "Long is a dedicated artist," says one, "and she enjoys the advantage of a wonderful singing tone." Mei also commands an enthusiastic following.

After you've watched and listened to several Cantonese operas you begin to understand the problems and pleasures involved. The singing consists of fixed and non-fixed tunes. Fixed tunes, with their easy rhythms and melodies, were introduced about fifty years ago as a way of winning bigger audiences. It's the better known among these tunes which are included today in commercial tapes of *karaoke* programmes. The actors and actresses have to follow these tunes strictly (and even if they wanted to, they would find it hard to "adlib" with their own versions — a difficulty increased by the nine different tones of the Cantonese language). If the artists forget the lyrics or make mistakes with the words you may see them standing dumbly on the stage while the music plays on.

It's the non-fixed tunes that are the core of the performance and the real essence of operatic singing. The words are more important than the melody but the artists are not strictly bound; they are allowed great liberty of expression. They can improvise a tune, stay on a particular note for as long as they like and they are not obliged to sing phrases in the same way in each performance. In fact they take over the role of the composer. This makes things difficult for the orchestra. The musicians have to guess how the tune of a particular singing part will go and cooperate instantly with the artist's voice. Usually they manage so well that the audience is unaware of it.

Newcomers sometimes object that this kind of singing can be too long-drawn-out, to the detriment of the operatic story and the action; but connoisseurs find it fascinating. Non-fixed tunes reveal talent and temperament. In one of her performances Long sang a seven-character phrase (known as "rolling flowers") in the wrong order but instantly put things right with the phrase that followed. It was done in a second.

"You can't expect an artist to remember every single phrase in a four-hour-long opera," says a critic. "In fact the audience is keenly entertained by this improvisation of the libretto and freedom to interpret, where Long excels. They'll come

This famous opera, *The Story of the Reincarnated Red Plum*, tells of a wicked prime minister, the beautiful concubine he pills, and the young scholar who loves her.

again and again to see the same opera performed and expect something different every time."

Cantonese opera has a special quality of involving the audience with the action on the stage. The actors, their eye make-up heavily expressive, turn to the auditorium for approval of their speech, commenting on the world outside — none of this to be found in non-Cantonese operas.

"Nowadays there's a growing respect for the opera and the artists," says a university teacher. "Not long ago young people would go only when they were taking their parents. Nowadays it's for their own enjoyment. Younger actors are performing and the productions are often magnificent. A high percentage of the audiences is under twenty-five. And the scenes of enthusiasm at the end are just like those after a pop concert — people rushing to the stage to take photos and press flowers and gifts on the artists."

A girl college student who went in for opera training ten years ago is now, as an amateur, performing regularly with local opera troupes. What made her do it?

"I was entranced by the delicacy of their interpretation," she says, "— that, and the wonderfully elaborate costumes and hair styles." She told how she and her friends would take blankets off the beds to make costumes with the traditional long sleeves and make twisted hairpins out of wire for the complicated coiffures. "A superficial interest if you like, but that was how it often started. Now we understand more and are deeply committed."

A young university lecturer Sau Y. Chan obtained his Ph.D. in the States but then returned to Hong Kong and studied opera, specializing particularly in the Cantonese form. "When I was studying in Hong Kong, opera was simply not in the syllabus. Yet I find in it invaluable traces of Chinese culture and the roots of local religious rituals. This is not just a study of aesthetics; it embraces anthropology, social philosophy and music."

Hong Kong's Urban Council and Regional Council have encouraged local opera. When a town hall has been opened in a new area it's meant more performances (both amateur and professional). The Councils also arrange discussion seminars and educational talks on opera, especially in Tsuen Wan Town Hall and in the same area the Sam Tung Uk Museum has frequent exhibitions of costumes and operatic materials.

You may hear in Hong Kong about Teochew opera. It is performed at the time of the Hungry Ghosts, which is the great festival of the Teochew people. Nowadays it closely resembles Cantonese opera (except that it's spoken and sung in the Teochew dialect) but years ago it was sung and acted entirely by children. They had to memorize the libretti of anything up to fifty operas so that one could be staged (to celebrate a wedding or anniversary) only a few days after it was chosen by the client.

Tales of savage treatment were common. The young performers were beaten if they forgot their lines and beaten if the applause was especially enthusiastic, to stop them suffering from swelled heads.

In the mid-1950s the office of Protector of Children in Singapore was largely occupied with looking after Teochew opera troupes. However this has all vanished and no one in Hong Kong these days seems to have heard of child opera, apart from a few specialist scholars.

Cantonese opera is an indelible part of Hong Kong life. Why does it not enjoy the same popularity across the border? "It's simply that the human scene is so different," said a student. "Guangzhou is just like Hong Kong twenty years ago — people looking practically into life, working hard to make a living … whereas in Hong Kong, people are more 'stable', and can afford the spare time and money to focus on something that they like."

To discourage the evil prime minister's advances the concubine double-plays the nymphomaniac, touches his beard, and feigns madness.

Chapter 16

Chinese Superstition

After Westerners have penetrated the Chinese world for some months they may begin to suspect that the people around them are somewhat superstitious. This is a monumental under-assessment. Superstition is hardly the word for it. Most Chinese are aware of a whole universe of the unseen promoting positive and negative forces, *yin* and *yang*. Each contains the elements of its opposite, which means that interpretation of these unseen forces can be very complicated. For the sophisticated they represent a philosophical rendering of the universe — something of often compelling interest but not to be taken too seriously. Simple people

The temple of Wong Tai Sin, in Kowloon, thronged everyday by amahs, shopkeepers, businessmen seeking guidance from the immortals in facing the future.

At Wong Tai Sin the smoke of essence rises as clients insert the joss sticks into the tripods and pay their respects to the immortal.

have learned a great deal about the unseen world and take it very seriously indeed.

Crystal-ball-gazing and fate-alleviating rites and procedures are part of the private lives of millions.

A Chinese businessman I know well is said not even to get his haircut without first ringing his soothsayer to know what date and time would be most auspicious. A bright young girl says, giving you a lucky charm to wear on a journey to Europe, "Yes, yes. I know (laughing) it's all a lot of nonsense, but still, wear it anyway." And when her friend met with an accident, inquired with concern whether she was wearing the charm at the time.

An acquaintance takes you up a backstreet to visit a woman fortune-teller with an ordinary everyday face, sitting behind a desk. "It's a great pity," she says, "that all this professional examination of the future was not taken up and studied scientifically and logically in universities and other places of scholar-

At Wong Tai Sin you find guidance to the future by shaking a stick from a jar and exchanging it for a red slip, the interpretation of which is to be found in a special book—which can be purchased for a small sum of money.

ship and research. For there is not the least doubt of its value and validity. Unfortunately it's never been properly recognized."

Since the 1984 Sino-British Joint Declaration and the certainty of being handed over to the Mainland was confirmed, Hong Kong people have become more concerned about the fate of themselves and their families, and fortune-telling, always an important part of Hong Kong life, is raking in the money today as never before. Practitioners follow various techniques to establish contact — holding hands, touching the client's cheek, or just eye-to-eye engagement. The first part of the session usually consists of an analysis of the client's character and circumstances. Some of it seems uncannily accurate. Then there comes the look at the future. Very often, some months later, it seems that important events foretold by the soothsayer did really come to pass. The inaccurate parts of the forecast (and sometimes they prove absurdly wrong) tend to be forgotten.

The fortune-teller establishes eye-to-eye contact or by looking at the clients palm.

Chinese set great store by the horoscope — portents based on observation of the planets and other heavenly constellations at moments in their orbits when they are in a certain relationship with each other, especially their positions at the time of a person's birth. A Chinese astrologer operating in San Francisco and held in the highest esteem by a large Hong Kong clientele, requires only the date and time of birth and a cheque for two thousand dollars, and by return of post comes the forecast. Astrology has its mass following in Hong Kong, but if the actual time-of-day of your birth isn't known, then you can expect only a vaguer picture.

Some of the local practitioners combine fortune-telling with *feng shui*, or geomancy. One man will actually calculate your fate only on the basis of the characters of your name, which he will if necessary take down over the phone. Many Hong Kong people feel it's important to know what days are auspicious for making a business deal, getting married or going on a

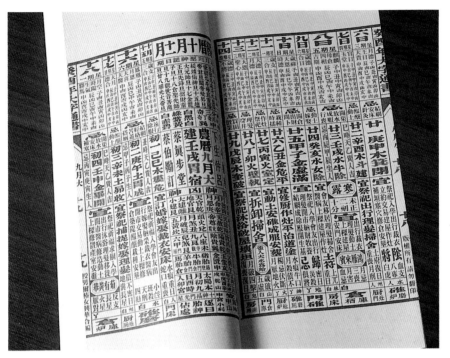

On this page of the *Farmer's Almanach* you may read that this is a good day for cleaning out the kitchen and getting a haircut.

journey, etc. Here the *Farmer's Almanach* comes into play. It is consulted by the older generation of Hong Kong working people and especially by villagers out in the New Territories.

This *Almanach* started out as a local publishing venture giving advice to farmers on the best planting and harvest times and other agricultural wisdom. Gradually its annual editions came to include such information as the best time for the big decisions of life, such as emigration and a daughter's marriage. It even gave advice on the pronunciation of English and on business methods followed in the urban areas. Nowadays several similar publications compete with the *Farmer's Almanach*.

Numbers and mathematics play a strange part in dealing with the unseen. Geomancers work out complicated equations using special compasses and elaborate measuring equipment with concentric circles; fortune-tellers some-times play with columns of figures.

Numbers can become particularly important simply because of their sounds when spoken. The word "four" is like the sound for "dead" in Chinese, so four is an unlucky number. Some hotels do not have a fourth floor designated as such. At the time of the recent landslides in southern Hong Kong, when two people lost their lives, the building directly affected was number forty-four Bagiuo Villas. What else could you expect?

The figure eight on the other hand is very felicitous. It is the same sound as the Cantonese word for "prosper". Car numbers are officially auctioned and the ones with plenty of eights arouse determined bidding and bring in sizable sums to the Hong Kong Government's coffers. The numbers three and nine are also propitious. Number two is acceptable, but certainly not four.

Some makes of European cars, although thoroughly reliable, sell poorly in the Hong Kong Chinese community, simply because the sound of their name in Chinese suggests something downbeat or derogatory like "finish" or "evacuation", and the Chinese businessman feels he's better off without them.

Advertising men in local firms attend special classes where they learn how to avoid unlucky names. The translation of a brand name from English to Chinese may decide success or failure in the local shops.

Until recently life insurance was very unpopular in Hong Kong. When a Hong Kong executive was about to leave for New York and his wife inquired whether it wouldn't be prudent to take out a policy, he rounded on her angrily, asking whether she wanted him dead. It seemed to him a most glaring way of tempting fate.

However even in the last three years the situation has been changing. Persistent reports on television and in the press of high-jacking, terrorist attacks, outbreaks of wars and rebellions, accidents to aircraft, have made the world seem a much less secure place. Prudence is a called for. Nowadays it's much more common for Chinese travellers to take out insurance for a journey though, as a salesman admitted the other day, it's still uphill work to sell a life policy to a white-collar Chinese worker, because of the lingering suspicion that it may be tempting fate. There is the same superstition towards the drawing up of a will as the term itself suggests the imminence of death. Most Chinese people have died without one, including some of the very rich and famous.

With this number-plate, you can expect the smile of fortune.

Fights in court over who should get what were therefore not uncommon.

Here in the Far East superstition shows itself much more obviously in everyday life. Westerners in close contact with Chinese people sometimes find themselves influenced by local attitudes. They find themselves reading more about telepathy, parapsychology, and also recent researches in the United States which seem to indicate that will-power can affect the outcome of events. The growing feeling is: "There may be something in it."

A British businessmen had paper kitchen gods stuck to the walls of the kitchen shortly before Chinese New Year. Both of them mysteriously became detached and slipped to the floor in the night. His wife was due to leave for Europe on a visit the next day, but he persuaded her not to go.

In fact nothing happened to the aircraft but, as he said, you can never be quite, quite sure. The longer you live in Hong Kong, the more you tend to feel that Chinese superstition may not be something to be dismissed all that lightly.

Chapter 17

Feng Shui

The Westerner, if he wants to avoid annoying his Chinese hosts, is well advised not to laugh or poke fun at *feng shui. Feng shui* (literally: "wind and water") is a mystery concerned with the siting, in harmony with the Unseen, of graves, houses, offices and other buildings, and the furnishing of rooms.

For many it is the magical link between man and the landscape, the formula which links him with his environment.

The basic idea is to ensure exposure to favourable winds and discourage evil spirits. How much of it is common sense and how much superstition? Where hides the shadow line between true *feng shui* and charlatanism? The important factor is that so many Chinese people take it more than half-seriously. "I don't know about spirits,"

The geomancer's compass is an instrument of mystery to the layman but it may profoundly influence the siting of a village or bank building.

says a large-scale developer like Gordon Wu, "but I respect *feng shui*. You want to feel comfortable in a building."

Any businessman knows that if his working environment is wrong because of vaguely hostile influences (bad *feng shui*), it may cost him dearly in money and lost goodwill. In an office in the business heart of Hong Kong, if the staff keep falling ill and orders diminish, then it is time to call in the *feng shui* expert. He may advise the boss to move his desk to a very inconvenient position near the doorway to his room and install a tank with six black fish. One office entrance may have to be closed and a new one opened in another wall. Highly inconvenient, but better than a staff walkout.

Is there something in the atmosphere of Hong Kong that gradually invades the disbelief of newcomers? It was a British factory owner who recalled how on two occasions when things were going badly, a Chinese business contact had suggested bad *feng shui* was at the root of it; and when he had made the necessary adjustments, profits picked up again.

Once he was told "Your luck is all running away with the water down that pipe from the printing works overhead, taking surface water across the pavement into the gutter." He called in the Urban Services and had it diverted.

The next time it was a question of all his profit rushing past over a new overhead road outside the factory. The answer was a mirror to turn back the flow of cash. It fell down several times but at last it was made to stick. Then the profits rose again.

Some entrepreneurs will consult the *feng shui* expert (sometimes known as the geomancer) about the positioning of a new office block they plan to build. There is no more convinced believer in the mystery than your conservative Cantonese businessman bred in a Mainland village, where the people have always known that the way you site houses and ancestral graves can mean all the difference between a peaceful life and crippling misfortune.

Feng shui means compliance with the laws of existence. The missionary writer Ernest Eitel thought that the Chinese "see a golden thread of spiritual lie running through every form of existence and binding together, as in a living body, everything in heaven and earth."

You ask whether there is a modern scientific basis for all this. "What has today's science to do with it?" a young Chinese University graduate asks. "It is simply there and can't be ignored. Maybe in a few hundred years from now the West may come up with scientific explanations. In any case it makes sense, surely, to achieve harmony with one's surroundings and (after listening to the *feng shui* expert) arrange the family home, the graves, the places of work, in an agreeable and propitious way?"

The large glass opening over the third floor main lobby at Exchange Square. It still failed to ensure good *feng shui* and prevent the stock exchange crash of 1987.

An ideal site for a home or village, so the *feng shui* experts say, is on higher ground facing the sea or a river and protected from cold winds by a

Statue at Exchange Square shows indulgence in *tai chi*, a form of martial arts.

horse-shoe of hills. Choose the land with care and, to make success doubly sure, placate the spirits of the earth with offerings. In the towns and cities, as far as they can, the builders follow the same guidelines. Any countryman will tell you that interference with the *feng shui* — changing the landscape through inauspicious digging of reservoirs or bulldozing roads through the hills — may be a very serious matter. If any man or beast falls sick, that must be because of the *feng shui* disturbance. A Christian convert once said, "When any villager builds a house he must choose a lucky day and employ priests to drive away evil spirits. We, believing in Jesus, refuse to do this. But then if any of the villagers are taken sick and die, the responsibility for the death is laid at our door."

It's one thing to call in the *feng shui* expert, but quite another to do what he lays down. A big local canning firm, about to auction off its assets, was told to make changes in the ballroom of the Hilton Hotel, where the auction was

One of the two great bronze lions outside the Hongkong and Shanghai Bank. *Feng shui* experts were consulted in their positioning to the north of the new building.

to be held. They shifted the bar and would have arranged to have the double-doors taken off their hinges and removed but the hotel management regretted this was impossible. The auction went well enough but not as well, the directors felt, as if there had been a wide-open doorway.

The developers of the great new Exchange Square towers were told by their geomancer that if good luck were to enter the building, the most auspicious way would be through a hole in the roof of the lobby. The architects settled for a large, glass-covered opening over the main lobby on the third floor. But the new Hong Kong Stock Exchange is on the ground floor — two levels below. How was the luck to get down to the brokers? It was asking too much to punch more holes in roofs and floors. As the opening of the new Exchange was soon followed by a boom period, the concern of doubters was quietly forgotten. But the *feng shui* expert murmurs: "Don't say I didn't warn you …" Lo and behold, scarcely a year after the Exchange's grand opening with much fanfare, Black

Monday struck and a few months after that the chairman of the Exchange was charged with offences under the Anti-Corruption Ordinance.

When the British first came to Hong Kong, they knew nothing about *feng shui*. Sometimes they brought calamities on themselves through their ignorance; sometimes the locals was deeply impressed by their seeming geomantic erudition. In *feng shui* lore, a range of hills is likened to a dragon and when the road was cut from Central out to Happy Valley, a dragon's back was broken and the bare red earth was his blood flowing. So no Chinese was surprised when fever carried off the Westerners who tried to turn Happy Valley into a residential area.

On the other hand, a most promising site from a *feng shui* point of view is Government House. It is screened at the back by the trees and terraces of the Botanical Gardens and is skirted by roads with graceful curves, safeguarding it from evil spirits which, as we know, can travel only in straight lines.

Downhill from Government House the benevolence of the Unseen continues, and surprisingly includes the Hongkong and Shanghai Bank with its two great bronze lions. They were shipped up to Japan in World War Two to be melted down; but somehow they escaped and Allied Occupation troops found them in an Osaka junk yard. So they returned home to Hong Kong and the bank's geomancer chose their careful placement on the north side of the grand new building. As he patiently explained: " The money flows straight into the bank, through the plaza and up the hill, and then floods back again into the bank. But if the lions were not there, it would all go out into the harbour." No one who has seen the Hongkong and Shanghai Bank's fortunes surge from strength to strength would disagree with him. Yet even homes like Government House which enjoy outstanding *feng shui* can have their fortune changed by huge construction projects in the victimity. Demolition work, piling and the digging up of roads are all supposed to change the *feng shui* of the offices or homes closest to them. And when the new building next to your office has protruding cutting edges, beware, for bad luck is at hand. When the new Bank

The tall new Bank of China building threatened the *feng shui* of Government House, which it was hoped would improve again after a tree was planted in the appropriate part of the garden.

of China building went up, and the edge of the building pointed at Government House like the blade of a sword, the *feng shui* of Government House changed from excellent to mediocre. There have been two changes of Governors since in spite of the planting of trees and other remedial action. When that beautiful building on number nine Queen's Road Central went up and its rugged edges pointed in the direction of the Bank of Credit and Commerce International, the bank went into liquidation.

Eric Cumine, doyen of Hong Kong architects, tells the story of the *feng shui* elder across the border in Guangdong who predicted an earthquake for 10 April 1981. Whereupon four thousand men, women and children in Haifeng and Lufeng counties, fifty miles north of Hong Kong, loaded sixty-nine junks with food and water and set sail for Hong Kong and safety.

They were turned back in Joss House Bay by amazed police and immigration officials and their stories of approaching doom, after being checked at the Royal Observatory, were dismissed as a naive attempt at illegal entry.

On 9 April the earth shook — admittedly, one day early. It was not a serious quake but to simple people it seemed a kind of reassurance — that there's more in earth and heaven than is dreamed of by bureaucrats.

A new skyscraper arose at number nine Queen's Road and presented sharp edges to the Bank of Credit and Commerce (B.C.C.). The bank broke soon afterwards.

Chapter 18

Chinese Healing

Hong Kong spends millions on a health service which is far better than in most places in the Far East. If you're run over in the street or fall off a ladder and break your pelvis, an ambulance is very soon on its way to whisk you off to a hospital casualty department. And after they've joined up the pieces, return to normal may be hastened by sessions at the MacLehose Medical Rehabilitation Centre.

As in most big cities of the world, death and injuries are largely the

The alternative to Western-style medicine— the Chinese pharmacy. Many Chinese are convinced that the Western doctor's knowledge is limited, and they turn to traditional treatments.

result of road accidents — the gruesome price society is willing to pay for the convenience of door-to-door transport. Hong Kong also sees many accidents on construction sites. Industrial accidents continue at a high rate, despite frequent education campaigns directed at workers using dangerous machines who put piecework income above safety.

Critics say the Hong Kong health system has grown haphazardly and that there's great imbalance between the private and the public sectors. The private sector is where most of the doctors work and where most of the money is made. The public hospitals have most of the beds and equipment, but their junior doctors are overworked and they are short of more than a thousand nurses.

If you are employed by the Government, medical and dental treatment are free. Cost of treatment in government hospitals for the general public is still low though the public wards are overcrowded and there are long queues at some of the out-patient clinics. Private hospitals are expensive and so are doctors in private practice.

There is no children's hospital in Hong Kong. It's argued by the authorities that with modern medicine costing millions, it makes more sense to treat child-patients in wards attached to the main hospitals and avoid duplicating equipment and facilities. The result from the children's point of view has not been very comforting. Drab surroundings, brusque treatment by hardworked staff, archaic visiting hours — this situation has been humanized to some extent, but I've been told of children having nightmares over people in white.

However in other sectors Hong Kong is well ahead and its people benefit from the achievements of modern medicine in the Western world. Some of the world's worst killers have been vanquished. Smallpox has been eradicated, leprosy stopped, a cure found for tuberculosis, venereal diseases successfully treated. The discovery of penicillin meant a complete answer to many kinds

Chinese medicines are extracted from herbs, flowers, vegetables, and the bodies of birds and beasts.

of infection. Pneumonia is no longer a dreaded disease. Insulin has been isolated, which means that diabetes is no longer a threat to the life of the sufferer. Knowledge of vitamins has led to their effective use against pellagra, beriberi and other nutritional illnesses. And for many years now patients suffering from cataracts have been able to have their sight restored.

Yet despite all these advances of Western medical science, only about twenty-five per cent of the illnesses that bring a patient to a doctor are successfully treated by Western drugs and procedures. The rest of the patients either get better by themselves, or succumb, or improve through individual treatment by a physician. So the doctor may be using his own experience and knowledge of the patient, and (in the Far East including Hong Kong) the world of herbs and other organic substances.

Indeed, as many Chinese will tell you, there is still a large area of suffering modern Western medicine has no answer for. They don't despise Western treatments, but they say these have limitations.

Hong Kong is in a peculiar situation. Its recognized doctors are trained in Western-style medical schools and have learned Western-type theories and practice. The public, nearly all Chinese, has the choice between Western and Chinese treatment, based on widely differing approaches to medicine and healing.

The newcomer to the territory is likely to hear about Chinese medicine through social contacts. The subject usually surfaces during dinner table conversation, in the form of an experience related by a sufferer who, after getting limited satisfaction from Western trained physicians, takes the advice of some Chinese friend and consults a herbalist or acupuncturist, and is cured within weeks. Many of these stories are well-founded.

Several thousand Chinese-style doctors, or herbalists as they are some-times called, are practising in Hong Kong; but the Government doesn't itself provide any traditional Chinese medical service, nor does it control those who do. So quality varies widely.

A Western wife who had suffered badly from hepatitis was told by her Western doctor that she was about eighty per cent back to normal and that was all that could be hoped for. She went to a recommended Chinese physician and he prescribed various medicines, one after the other, in an experimental approach. The ingredients, bought at a Chinese pharmacy, invariably pro-duced a repulsive-tasting pitch-black brew, which the patient bravely swallowed. In time the doctor found the right answer, and she has felt normal and healthy ever since.

In this case the Westerner was advised by Chinese friends and consulted a Chinese practitioner held in high esteem in the Chinese community for his

The Chinese-style doctor often has his surgery on the pharmacist's premises, where prescriptions are made up following consultation.

skills in diagnosis.

Yet a Western woman who underwent acupuncture for a strained wrist was surprised that it showed no improvement. Then her own doctor saw that it was a fracture, not a sprain, so needles would do no good. Yet acupuncture (application of needles to special areas of the body) when carried out by an experienced operator is widely accepted as an effective healing method in certain cases. Related to acupuncture is acupressure, where a form of massage is used instead of needle insertions; and moxibustion (the application of smouldering plant leaves).

How can the outsider be sure of finding the right Chinese physician? Only by careful inquiries among Chinese friends and acquaintances.

A Chinese friend said: "A good ninety per cent of herbal doctors and acupuncturists are simply former assistants in pharmacies or surgeries who've picked up knowledge as they went along. The genuine doctors, the good ones, are usually old and are besieged by patients. When you go to see them, even with an appointment, you may have to wait for hours."

Chinese-style doctors are still being trained on the Mainland. A really good herbalist will know something like three hundred prescriptions. One woman we know in Guangzhou (Canton) studied Western medicine for five years at Sun Yat Sen Medical University. Then she studied Chinese (herbal) medicine for four years, and acupuncture (including acupressure) for another two, at the university hospital.

If you ask Chinese friends about the relative merits of herbal and Western medicine, their replies vary. Chinese patients like to see results within twenty four hours; otherwise they will rapidly seek a second opinion.

"If it's a fracture or some operation like appendicitis, I'd be inclined to go to a Western hospital," said a Chinese businessman, "but Chinese are very aware that there's a whole area of medicine where the Western-trained doctor cannot help much — I am thinking now particularly of back pains and some types of cancer. If Western medicine doesn't provide much relief, then I would certainly try my herbalist. And sometimes Chinese bone-setters are very good at dealing with dislocations and sprains."

A young Chinese businessman whose attractive wife was dying of inoperable cancer said wistfully: " There's a man in Kowloon who says he can cure a case like my wife's. But he's asking two hundred thousand dollars and I think he's a fake."

A Chinese pharmacist said with various internal complaints Western drugs could be very effective if you wanted quick results. The negative aspect of this was the danger of side-effects. On the other hand, if you were prepared to be patient, Chinese herbal remedies might in the long run do you more good, for they were aimed at a general gentle improvement of the whole body's mechanism. "Westerners sometimes joke about the use of rhinoceros and deer horns as aphrodisiacs," he said, "but the truth is, they are used as ingredients of prescriptions aimed at a general 'bucking-up' effect, not just sexual prowess. Apart from these extensive use is made of roots and leaves whose efficacy has been tested."

What are these plants? The Chinese have produced an enormous pharmacopoeia — mostly the work of a famous physician, Li Shizhen. He travelled on foot over many of China's mountains where medicinal plants were to be found, and studied their growth and properties. He spent twenty-seven years on his *Compendium of Materia Medica* and revised it three times. The final work contains a million characters and describes in detail 1,800 kinds of medicinal plants. He died just before it was printed.

It is very difficult for Western experts to assess the importance of herbal medicine. The root ginseng, for instance, is prized throughout the Far East as a tonic with amazing powers to arrest the ageing process and generally improve the bodily condition of older people. Yet medical analysis reveals no obvious explanation for ginseng's efficacy.

The criticism most often levelled against herbal medicines is that, because practitioners are unregistered, it's not possible to check the drugs used and to monitor treatment.

" That's true," says your Chinese friend, "but you can't deny that people who've been using herbal remedies for four thousand years, cutting out those which prove useless or harmful and promoting those that get results, are likely to end up with some useful prescriptions.

"We can't supply articles to the learned journals explaining why a certain plant or combination of plants improves a patient's condition. It's empirical — a question of trial and error down the centuries."

When the Communists took over the Mainland, they began by introducing Western medicine, but soon were brought face to face, in the early 1950s, with the enormous cost of providing a Western-type national health service for half a billion people. So they promoted traditional medicine and the whole world learned about the amazing results achieved by acupuncture. The practice of inserting needles at points known as meridians had a relationship with the working of the nervous system but could not be precisely defined. In the early 1970s the use of acupuncture to replace anaesthesias for operations was much publicized, and great claims were made for the new methods. Later its importance was down-graded, and it was admitted that as far as anaesthesia was concerned, acupuncture was useful in not more than ten per cent of cases. Still no one quite knows why it works. Certainly it seems to stimulate the production of certain morphine-like substances in the brain. It's been substituted for conventional anaes-thesia in a limited number of amputations and operations on the head, throat and lungs — but not below the waist.

However this doesn't mean that a good Hong Kong or Mainland acupuncturist may not be able to work wonders with an aching muscle or rheumatic hip.

Once you become really interested in Chinese medicine, you enter a world where words like superstition, folklore, magic are no longer valid. It is simply a different world. There you make your first encounter with the ancient Daoist origins of *yin* and *yang*. According to ancient Chinese teaching, *yin* and *yang* are the basis not only of medicine, but of the entire universe. Negative is *yin*, positive is *yang*. Cold is *yin*, hot is *yang*. Night is *yin*, day is *yang*. Every object around us, every aspect of our existence can be seen in terms of *yin* and *yang*.

You will soon be hearing about something called "*qi*" — vital energy. *Qi* is what differentiates life from death. For the maintenance of health, there must be a balance of *qi* — neither too little nor too much. There are three origins of *qi*: original *qi*, that part which is transmitted to you by your

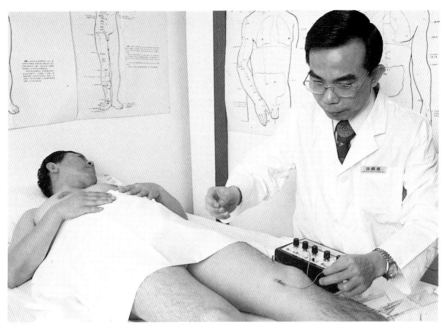

Acupuncture—insertion of needles at various key points of the body—is one of the older known Chinese medical treatments.

parents; nutritional *qi* derived from the food you eat; and, thirdly, the *qi* derived from the air you breathe. When all these are in balance, you are resistant to disease and no harm will come to you.

Because Chinese medicine emphasizes the personal element and the relationship between doctor and patient, it tends to be non-generalized and hard to monitor.

At present the Hong Kong authorities are carrying out an inquiry into Chinese medicine in Hong Kong. There have been cases (well-publicized by the authorities) in the last two years of Chinese herbal remedies proving fatal when maladministered. At the same time demand has grown for Chinese medicine to be recognized as a serious alternative to Western practice here; and Chinese in Hong Kong continue to consult Chinese medicine before they approach the Western physicians, or if the Western trained physician seems not to have the answer to their problems. The careful patient will, as always, seek a Chinese practitioner of high repute for that second opinion.

Chapter 19

Gambling
and the
Jockey Club

You hear a great deal in Hong Kong about people ruined and families disrupted by dangerous drugs, but you never seem to hear about families ruined through gambling.

It's a most extraordinary example of double standards sanctioned by the establishment; for the dedicated gambler — the kind of man who will sell all the family furniture in the final stages of his passion — causes just as much suffering among Hong Kong people as in any other community. "When you think of marrying," said a Hong Kong girl worker, "there are four big vices you have to be on guard against in your intended husband. They are women, gambling, drink and narcotics. And the worst of these is gambling. You fall in love, get married, and then find he's two hundred thousand in debt to the illegal bookies. It's a terrible shock. All your life-style expectations change."

Lively finish at a race meeting at Sha Tin, one of the most modern race-courses in the world.

Horse racing, and betting on the race-results, are part of life here — and firmly backed and approved by the powers-that-be. The controlling body is the Royal Hong Kong Jockey Club, which enjoys enormous prestige and influence. More people belong to the Jockey Club than to any political party in Hong Kong. It used to be said that the Club wielded the top influence in the running of Hong Kong, followed by the Hongkong and Shanghai Bank and the Governor (in that order). Governors have led the Club's list of patrons; leaders of commerce and industry (along with humbler men) have owned champions and losers.

The cash turn-over from race meetings is enormous. About HK$25 billion is betted on the horses every year by Hong Kong people — that is about HK$3,500 for every man, woman and child in the colony. But the Club is not run for profit. After expenses have been met (including government taxes) the rest of the takings are spent on charitable and other projects benefiting the Hong Kong public.

It's not surprising that Hong Kong seems mad on the races. The two racecourses — at Happy Valley and Sha Tin — offer almost the only legal means of betting in the Colony, apart from the official Mark Six lottery, which is also run by the Jockey Club.

Northern Chinese, while admitting a traditional interest in horses and horse racing going back to the famous Tang dynasty (618–907), have self-righteously deplored the prevalence of betting here and decry it as a Southern Chinese vice; though once they come down to settle here in Hong Kong they soon seem to catch the fever.

Some people bet after carefully studying the records of the horses and their riders and trainers. Some consult soothsayers and racing correspondents writing in the local press, others are influenced by the favourable omens suggested by horses' names.

More than a dozen newspapers are devoted entirely to horse racing and many more give up pages to it. Strangely enough a number of papers carry forecasts of the lottery results, basing the likely winning combinations on numbers already chosen or left out of previous draws. Superstition is deep-rooted. When a punter goes to Happy Valley or Sha Tin, he always likes to

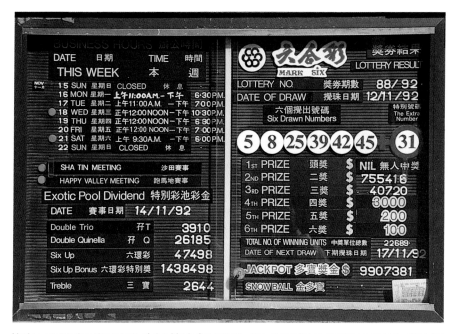

Notice anouncing the result of the Mark Six lottery, one of the legal gambling opportunities for Hong Kong people.

keep to one particular area. It is supposed to be extremely unlucky to be greeted or approached from behind. *Feng shui* and geomancy are important to the Hong Kong racing world. There are offerings to Heaven and ceremonies conducted by priests when the track is returfed or important changes made in the layout; or after bad accidents.

The huge amounts staked on the performance of one horse arouse almost irresistible temptations to make that horse win or lose by irregular means. The Club goes to great lengths to keep local racing clean. Stipendiary stewards police the race meetings, every yard of every race is filmed. Horses are tested before and after every race for dope. The Club's security department has the job of knowing what's going on in the local racing world and sifting the gossip. However it's difficult to be a hundred per cent certain that bribes are never paid and races never fixed. And in any case nothing is likely to curb the enthusiasm of Hong Kong punters.

Do any declared opponents of racing and betting exist in Hong Kong? You might meet some, among church and social workers, but even they are fatalistic. The Jockey Club is above criticism. Who is going to attack an organization which, after expenses have been met, pays out millions for a whole spectrum of public welfare projects — from polyclinics, schools and training centres to swimming pools, sports grounds, a new university and the great oceanarium and other attractions of Ocean Park?

Hong Kong people's love of gambling doesn't stop at horse racing. There's also gambling at mah-jong, fan-tan, crickets fighting and anything else you can bet on — all of which is illegal here. But it's all allowed in Macau, the small Portuguese-run territory fifty miles to the West across the Pearl River estuary. Untold thousands travel to Macau to gamble in its casinos. You can be there by jet-foil within the hour. You'll hear of wayward wives of Hong Kong businessmen seeing their husbands off to the office, then hurrying to Macau, losing twenty thousand by teatime before returning to Hong Kong to greet their beloveds with winning smiles and nobody the wiser — until the bank statement at the end of the month.

When humbler people lose their money the loan-shark is waiting. Loan-sharking — money-lending at astronomical rates of interest — is the great social curse of Hong Kong. It's against the law but many people, once in the loan-sharks' clutches, are too frightened to go to the police. And if there's one thing loan-sharks have developed, it's the art of inspiring fear. Debt collection in Hong Kong often degenerates into strong-arm tactics and violence.

What will happen to the gambling scene in Hong Kong after the 1997 take-over? What does the future hold for the Jockey Club? When you recall how the Communists stamped out gambling on the Mainland after they won power in 1949, you might think chances of its surviving in Hong Kong are none too bright. However we are living in a time of Deng Xiaoping-style economic reform, when local officials are urged to borrow ideas from capitalism when it invigorates the masses and stimulates production. Racing has already begun in Guangzhou, and there are plans to renew and reactivate at least one of the two courses in Shanghai, once the centre of social life in the days of "semi-colonialism," later surviving as public parks.

The Royal Hong Kong Jockey Club has developed friendly relations with Mainland officials and has given much appreciated advice on organization, training and finance. So far as racing is concerned, it looks as though nothing will be allowed to interfere with Hong Kong's capitalist life-style.

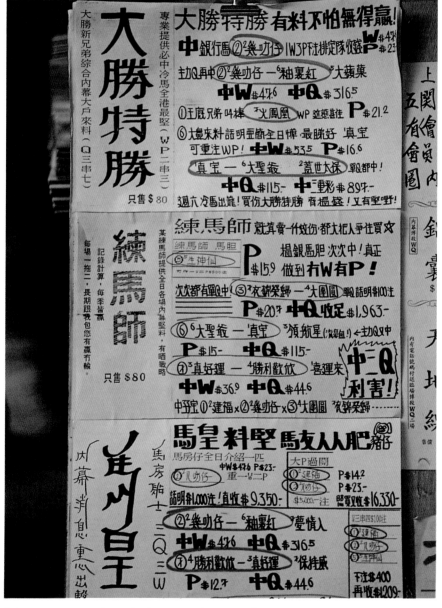

Sale of racing tips is a flourishing industry in Hong Kong. This paper gives you three certain winners and reminds you of this tipster's past unerring choices.

Chapter 20

Welcome Guests? Well...

By and large Hong Kong people are highly suspicious of outsiders wanting to come and live here, especially when they arrive without money. This is a small place, it's argued, and large influxes of foreigners (especially Vietnamese) fleeing their own country are a nuisance at best and, too often, a strain on resources and a threat to the peace.

Nor does Hong Kong offer a particularly neighbourly welcome to compatriots coming from the China Mainland. As for the great army of

They arrived in their scores of thousands after the Communists took over Vietnam. They came in leaking fishing boats, in packed freighters. Hong Kong never turned any away.

Filipinos in domestic service, they are often regarded as a necessary evil, useful for the work they do but too conspicuous on their free days, crowding the public squares, filling the air with their animated trading and swapping of experience like thousands of birds, and leaving unacceptable quantities of litter.

However the strangers offering most headaches for Hong Kong have been the Vietnamese. Unlike the Filipinos they have wanted to leave their country for good; although it must be admitted their aim has rarely been to stay in Hong Kong; but rather to make for the United States or, (if that fails) other Western countries.

Vietnamese have been coming to Hong Kong for thirty years or more — ever since the civil war between the government forces and the Communists began to warm up and young men were conscripted into the army. Young Vietnamese of Chinese origin would seek refuge in Hong Kong while planning a further move to the West (in those days that usually meant France). When the Communist armies overran the South and the government of President Thieu collapsed, the refugee flow to Hong Kong became a flood overnight. At first the local reaction was sympathetic. In 1975 although a Royal Visit was due next day and the preparations took time and attention, Ghurka units still worked through the night preparing army camps for the Vietnamese arrivals, and there were many declarations of goodwill and a desire to help.

However when the packed boats kept coming with their hundreds and thousands of asylum-seekers, public sympathy dried up.

Hong Kong is a generous place; however it is one thing to make out a cheque to Oxfam to help allay hunger in Africa but quite another to vote millions of dollars' year after year, to build new Vietnamese security camps and pay for the growing expenses, even if the United Nations High Commission for Refugees shoulders the main burden.

Voices were soon raised demanding that Vietnamese boat people be loaded on one big chartered ship and sent back to where they belonged. Hong Kong is just not big enough to house them, was the cry. They fall sick, they have babies, they take up hospital beds and treatment and deprive our

Prison type camps housed the unwelcome guests. The aim was to deter others from coming, but they still arrived by the boat load. Now at last the flow has stopped.

own people of medical care. Besides, even the American government repatriates Haitians, don't they? But what about the awful risks they have taken in order to reach Hong Kong, the tales of pirate attacks in the Gulf of Thailand, the raping of women, robbing of jewellery, sinking of boats? Well, nobody asked them to put to sea; it was their choice. End of argument.

Under an international agreement reached in Geneva in 1979, Hong Kong was supposed to be a place of first asylum — that is to say, a temporary refuge from which Western countries would take regular quotas of boat people for resettlement. However Western countries (including Britain but with Norway as an honourable exception) reneged on the terms of the agreement and the numbers behind steel fences in Hong Kong grew by the tens of thousands. Hong Kong never turned boat people away, as did some other Asian countries including Singapore. The Hong Kong policy was rather one of "humane deterrence" — providing conditions of minimal subsistence and comfort, in the hope that the message would soon filter back to the Vietnam coastal countryside and that would-be refugees would be dissuaded from risking a perilous voyage. Under a screening process about ten per cent of the boat people in the Hong Kong camps were designated as true refugees; those screened out would be condemned as "economic migrants" coming not in fear of persecutions but simply in search of an easier life.

However for some years these policies seemed to be getting nowhere. The Vietnamese kept coming, the Vietnamese authorities showed no willingness to take back "screened out" boat people, Western countries were reluctant to help with resettlement.

Gradually the impasse was overcome. The Vietnamese government agreed to take back a batch of boat people repatriated against their will. It made depressing TV coverage — men and women manhandled aboard the aircraft, kicking, resisting and crying out — but it was becoming clear now that a journey to Hong Kong simply meant a dead end. And for those in the Hong Kong camps, if you failed the screening process and also failed your appeal — "two wings to the chicken" as the saying went; then you might as well volunteer to return, especially as it was now agreed that Hong Kong money (and probably contributions from the European Community) would be spent on helping former boat people to start life again in the home town or village.

But there are more than forty thousand boat people still in camps in Hong Kong, many of them children, and even if there are no hitches it will probably take until 1997 to get rid of them all.

Modern mass migration is a strange and disquieting phenomenon. There was a time when the big cities of the world seemed to have plenty of room and families from abroad would enrich the local landscape with new attitudes and ideas, new techniques and art-forms. Migrants had said goodbye to their own countries; they were people rooting themselves in ideas rather than places; in memories as much as in material things. Nowadays the migrant is often a simple nuisance. The empty large countries — Canada and Australia — still

The boat people were given medical care and limited education for children and adults. Some social activities were organized.

Now that conditions are better in Vietnam, the hope is that more boat people will agree to return. But 40,000 prefer to stay.

offer a welcome but a crowded one like Britain even denies nationality to those born on British soil, let alone those of a different race.

The 90,000 Filipinos working in Hong Kong have one thing in common with the Vietnamese boat people — they have no desire to make Hong Kong their permanent home. Actually there is a Hong Kong quota for intending Vietnamese immigrants, but it is far from being filled. Vietnamese don't enjoy living among the Cantonese and anyway permanent entry requires satisfactory performance in a language test.

The Filipinos nearly all speak English; in a colony where English is part of the school curriculum, this helps to make them acceptable as servants. Their aim is to earn money to send back to their families in the Philippines, where poverty is widespread, especially in parts of the countryside and the slums of Manila. Hong Kong is by no means the only overseas place of work for Filipinos. Millions of dollars in hard currency flow regularly into the Philip-

Money-making, husband-and-wife-earning, Hong Kong depends heavily on a foreign domestic work force. Close on 90,000 women from the Philippines work in Hong Kong and throng the Central district on their Sunday day off.

pines from the wages of overseas workers in a dozen countries.

How the domestic service scene has changed here in Hong Kong! Fifteen years ago the Chinese amah in black and white was an essential part of Hong Kong life; now she has largely disappeared. Sometimes you will find her in resigned retirement in some home of the Little Sisters of the Poor, where her former employer has assured her a refuge by making welcome contributions to the Order in the past. The Chinese amahs, mostly from Shunde county in Guangdong province, were a very special, often formidable race with their own ideas of how a home should be run, taking it as an insult if the wife dared enter the kitchen. They worked hard and for long hours; but a new generation of possible successors has preferred a job in a shop, or even a factory. The growing army of Filipinos fills the gap and also serves the newly emerged middle class that has so transformed Hong Kong society. It's a strange and varied work force, including in its ranks trained teachers and nurses and other professional women, who come to Hong Kong to scrub and cook for wages higher than a university teacher would hope for back home. The general impression is that Filipinos working for Western families are usually happier. Chinese employers have a reputation of being tough and demanding. "You're at it from morning till night with little time for a chat." Reported cases of abuse are relatively few, though critics say this is because it's very difficult to get redress. The contracts for employing Filipinos are very strict and protective and include payment of fares back home; but if conditions of work are intolerable and the maid complains, she is likely to be sacked at once and although she can seek justice, the case may not be heard until after she has exhausted her allowed period of stay. And what does she live on while waiting for the case to be heard? A catch 22 situation, it would seem.

As a result of complaints, a large-scale survey is being carried out of the whole Filipino work situation in Hong Kong.

Much less is heard about Thais, Sri Lankans and others working in Hong Kong as domestics. Rumours are spreading of ill-treatment among them and gross flouting of laid-down wage-levels.

More fateful and historically important than any other arrivals in Hong Kong are those from the Mainland. More decisive than any consulate-general or commission is the Mainland's political presence in the Colony, in the form of the New China News Agency — Xin Hua. As everyone knows this is far more than a news-gathering organization; its six hundred employees are also engaged in all kinds of contacts and intelligence and its chief is an important spokesman for Beijing.

Even more important in the eyes of many local analysts is the Mainland's business presence. Representatives of many cities and provinces have offices here and conduct many kinds of business deals and joint operations. The People's Liberation Army is said to have an office here and to maintain contacts with foreign governments — potential customers for China-made hardware. Discussions with Taiwan are sometimes carried out in the Colony. It's not known just how many Mainland so-called township enterprises are active here or how many Hong Kong enterprises run on Mainland capital, but the figure is well into the thousands.

These days you hear far more Mandarin, or *putonghua* as it is now called, spoken in the streets and restaurants of Hong Kong by visiting officials, by long-term business representatives, and by many kinds of people who have left the Mainland for good.

For the ordinary migrants from the Mainland wanting to start a new life in Hong Kong, the welcome is cool. Seventy-five are allowed in legally every day, armed with exit permits from provincial authorities across the border. Just how these permits are obtained is a matter of connections and cash payments to demanding officials. The new arrivals are from many provinces and include women and children. Half of them speak only Mandarin and know nothing of the local Cantonese language. Some are well-educated, some simple villagers.

" You can tell they are Mainlanders," says a very middle-class Hong Kong Chinese acquaintance, indicating a group at a nearby table in the restaurant. " They have dark complexions; they have had their hair waved at the barber's; and their manners and language are simply awful."

Surely she was exaggerating? "Not at all," says an accountant friend. " I had Mainlanders move into the flats either side of me and after a few months I decided to move out, they were such unpleasant, noisy neighbours, with no consideration for anyone."

Some new arrivals are helped by relatives already in Hong Kong; others are confronted by daunting problems — finding a job, a place to live, schooling for the children and, more than anything, the inhuman frenzy of Hong Kong daily life. Children from village schools on the Mainland are usually at least two years behind their Hong Kong peers. Special classes organized by the Hong Kong branch of International Social Service have long waiting lists and urgently need more accommodation to cope with the backlog.

Growing numbers of Mainlanders come to Hong Kong by illegal means, packed in speedboats or below decks on smugglers' junks; or somehow finding their way past the wire fences and patrols along the Hong Kong–Mainland border. Most of them are young people from the villages, hoping to get work in Hong Kong, make some money, and then go home again to get married and set up house. The income you can hope to earn in rural Guangdong is as little as a tenth of the going rates in Hong Kong.

If illegals are caught soon after crossing the border, they are at once sent back. If they take a job (usually on a building site) and are caught working, they face sentences of eighteen months imprisonment. More than a third of all the prisoners in Hong Kong gaols are illegals caught working. It's a strange situation. Hong Kong employers here have persuaded the Government to allow foreign (which means Mainland) workers into the territory because of an allegedly acute labour shortage. Many thousands have come already, along with rumours of unscrupulous contractors pocketing a large percentage of the agreed wages, and of living accommodation well below regulatory standards. Meanwhile several thousand young men and women, wanting to work here but dodging the legal channels, sit in Stanley and other prisons before being sent back home with a barely deserved criminal record. The more sordid stories are of the conscienceless employer who takes on illegal Mainlanders and then, just as payday looms, tips off the police. In this way he gets several weeks' labour from village lads without having to pay for it. In recent months, employers have been taken to court for employing illegals but the fines imposed have hardly been a major deterrent.

Why do the illegals still try their luck against the patrols, frontier guards and Hong Kong police? Are there no factories where they come from? Indeed there are. Hong Kong manufacturing investment along the Pearl River Valley and throughout Guangdong and neighbouring areas has provided jobs, so it's asserted, for at least three million men and women — of course at low Mainland rates.

However three million jobs is not enough to take care of all those seeking work. Unemployment in the Mainland countryside is on a massive scale. Thousands of villagers (many from remoter provinces) arrive in Guangzhou railway station every week, hoping to be hired; although the authorities urgently persuade them to go home again and start enterprises in their own villages. Many of them, finding no hope around Guangzhou, move further south, in an effort to reach Hong Kong, which throughout China is regarded as a kind of *El Dorado*. Arthur Miller, directing his own play *Death of a Salesman* in Beijing asked the young Chinese actor, who played the part of the salesman's son, what he would say to his date if he wanted to impress her. The young actor replied, "I would tell her my father is in Hong Kong."

Some see all this as a foretaste of post-1997 for Hong Kong, when untold masses will seek to come here after China resumes sovereignty. However long before the hand-over Hong Kong will have to deal with a mushrooming problem of labour. How many thousands will be needed to build the new airport, the new container terminal, the housing estates, the developing service industries, the new hotels and plazas and shopping centres?

So far there's been little consultation with Hong Kong trade unions. Some friction was inevitable. The colonial authorities have shown their usual supportive attitudes to business and industry, whose record includes some lamentable examples of insensitivity to staff anxiety as well as lack of sense in personnel management. This at a time when the Hong Kong scene offers growing job opportunities in some sectors and elsewhere a need for streamlining.

For instance in 1991 Hong Kong Telephone Company suddenly dismissed 1,159 of its staff, smartly informing the company union that this move was "not negotiable". Profit for the year was more than two and a half billion dollars. Of course this kind of approach, if it succeeds, saves management a deal of time and trouble. Reaction in the coming years, you might expect, would be an angry labour militancy. But Hong Kong unions are mostly pro-Beijing who presumably will not favour labour troubles after 1997. Mainland CITIC (Chinese International Trust and Investment Corporation) owns 20% of Hong Kong Telecom which is the holding company of Hong Kong Telephone. Ironic? Hardly, stranger things have happened in Hong Kong which has been castigated by critics as a place where "anything goes and nobody cares."

More recently the strike of Cathay Pacific Airline flight attendants left a nasty taste in the mouth of the public. As usual in manning and pay disputes the rights and wrongs of the situation were hard for the laymen to unravel. What seemed obvious was the lack of prior consultation and the "take it or leave it" heavy-handedness of management, which scored a short-term success, but in the longer term …?

Chapter 21

Mixing and Mingling

Every week new joint ventures are launched in the new land of opportunity —Hong Kong and South China combined. New vistas open up. If the figures are right, China is into an economic revolution unknown before in the history of the world.

The country's foreign trade was up by twenty per cent for the first half of 1992 compared with the same six months in the previous year. Fifteen per cent of that was accounted for by the Special Economic Zones near Hong Kong.

What are the human aspects of these sweeping changes? Obviously China is becoming a different place, but it still has a totalitarian government and dissent is a criminal offence. This is a time of transition and contradictions, as visitors to the Mainland soon find out. These

To the arriving Westerner the Chinese world will be full of surprises, some disconcerting, some highly agreeable. Understanding this world will call for patience, goodwill and a sense of humour.

include growing numbers of tourists, who almost stopped coming after the 1989 Tiananmen crackdown but are now returning. Many are from Hong Kong. So there's an increasing two-way mingling of Chinese from both sides of the border, both looking at the future in new ways and with new concern.

Some things in China are slow to change. Tourists are unimpressed by the poor service in the shops and restaurants, the lack of politeness, especially in Beijing. "All because of the iron ricebowl," says a young Hong Kong student. "In a Hong Kong shop the assistant wants to do his job well, wants to sell you something. In a Mainland shop you're the suppliant, you have to persuade the assistant to give you some attention. For instance if you go into a shoe shop there, and ask to try on a pair, the people behind the counter will most likely be busy in conversation and are rather annoyed to be interrupted."

"Rather unwillingly they offer you a pair and when you've tried them on you ask to see another pair of slightly different style, and they say: 'What's the matter, isn't that pair good enough? They look all right to me'; and if you insist, they may turn really sour."

Hong Kong people know very well what life is like on the Mainland. When they visit Guangzhou (Canton) with their wads of dollars they are the equivalent, so to speak, of Western tourists penetrating the lively shopping areas of Kowloon. "Mainlanders know at once you're from Hong Kong," says a young business trainee, "something to do with the cut of your clothes or your general manner. Hong Kong people are not all that popular."

Young back-packers travel the Mainland the hard way, penetrate deeper into daily life, come to know the qualities of ordinary people — their good nature, curiosity, skills in survival and making-do — but also the red tape, the difficulty of buying a railway ticket except on the black market, the corruption, the rip-offs.

Group-tourists travelling more expensively leave with an abiding impression of journeys of thousands of kilometres between huge drab cities, famous landscapes and multicourse Chinese meals; but they won't learn much about the people. They will tend to judge China by their guides, whose quality varies with the importance of the visiting group. The bad guides are useless, however pleasant as human beings. Their command of English is as woefully inadequate as their local knowledge.

Among foreigners in China it's obviously the teachers and students staying for many months, rather than the tourists, who become familiar with Chinese ways and attitudes, hopes and fears. Anyone speaking Mandarin will return home with the memory of revealing conversations, impressions of a human, friendly, long-suffering people.

An American foreign language student tells how once on a crowded bus from Chengdu to Kunming in the Southwest, he started a conversation with the Chinese man sitting next to him. Whereupon the man stood up and made an announcement to the whole bus that there was a Chinese-speaking American

Westerners and Chinese still coexist rather than mingle, because their cultures and life styles are still far apart.

among them; and the language student was busy talking for the next two hours, asking and answering questions. What impressed him, he said, was that so many people now have enough money to travel and visit relatives and see something of their own vast country. And so many people are earning money on the side, beside the income from their official *danwei* (place of work).

As for their views on the United States these reflected the journalism of official propaganda. The American was asked about divorce, AIDS, crime, the plight of the poor, the chance to grow rich. Most would like to go there — to have a look, they said.

" The people are so pleasant but the living is so hard," said a young American girl who worked with a Beijing company. " The climate is terrible and there's very little heating or air-conditioning. And the inflation is bad — fifty *yuan* these days for a taxi from the outskirts into downtown Beijing. So you cycle everywhere; it takes hours."

"Office and factory workers in Beijing spend an enormous amount of time sitting around, drinking tea and gossiping. They don't rush at things to get them done, as we do in Hong Kong, or in the West."

"If you go on an errand somewhere in Beijing to collect some documents, say, you don't just cycle there, ask for the papers, collect them, and come back. No, you sit down and drink tea and have a chat first; it would be thought odd to do otherwise."

"What do they talk about? Oh, anything under the sun — politics, learning English, the world outside China. As an American I'm a great object of interest; but they already know a lot about the States, from books and TV This general chat, they call it *kan dashan* — " Talking the big mountain."

"But people still have to be careful when it comes to talking about themselves. There's a lot of gossiping and informing going on. I spent some time living in a university hostel where many Third World students were living, and they were very careful, for if they said anything too much out of line, they risked expulsion and the end of their careers back home. There were known spies; you saw them quietly making notes after people had been gossiping. The Sri Lankans were usually the spies."

"But by and large the Chinese themselves are a formidable lot. Many of them are so intelligent and when they work they really achieve results. If they ever got their act together, they would be right out in front of all the rest of us. It's a bit scary to think about. Perhaps it's just as well they mess things up politically as they do."

What about the contrast between the Mainland and Hong Kong? Western foreigners coming to Hong Kong on a short visit are often simply dazzled. Those who stay and work here enjoy many advantages but also have to face problems. Parents have sometimes found it very difficult to place their children in school; clubs' waiting lists are so long that it's time to return to London or Sydney before there's a vacancy. Wives become bored because they don't find enough to do. Even trained Western social workers may find it hard to find work in Hong Kong unless they can understand and speak Cantoneses.

Many interracial contacts develop in Hong Kong universities and colleges between Chinese teachers and foreign students. But how deep and how permanent? According to a Chinese woman teacher, relations with Western students are usually cordial so long as the course lasts, "but after that all

People may seek to understand the other community but looking in the bus window see only the reflection of their own set ways and attitudes.

friendships are forgotten, you never hear any more from them. That is not the Chinese way. With us the links between the teacher and the student are longlasting."

Interracial misunderstandings are most common at the lower levels where the language barrier is insuperable and local customs seem most offensive. Chinese women never cease to be astonished at the physical bulk of some Western girls and wives, the loudness of their laughter, their exaggerated gestures. On their side Westerners also find something to complain about. A lecturer on the Chinese was emphasizing the politeness of Chinese social relationships. A Western member of the audience asked whether he was talking about the same lot of people. "Have you seen them crowding the ferries in hordes on a Sunday, pushing and shoving and half-trampling you under foot?"

Situation and circumstance are decisive. Most Chinese are polite but it's focussed largely on family members and close friends. Non-Chinese people normally have it the other way around, to the astonishment of my Chinese acquaintance. An angry Chinese wife demanded of her Australian husband: "Why were you so unkind about my latest hairstyle and so polite to a complete stranger when you trod on her feet at the bus stop?"

Chapter 22

Neighbours All around You

Most Hong Kong families are living in tightly packed conditions. Do they mind this? What about the poetic figure in Chinese literature, the reflective man glad to dwell in some remote valley far from the bustle and corruption of the city, drinking with an old friend or meditating in solitude?

"I cannot really answer that," a busy young Hong Kong housewife confesses, "never having been one for solitude. Anyway here there is not much point in such ideas. In Hong Kong we are used to crowds and noise, and we quite like that. As soon as we come home to our housing-estate flat we turn on the TV whether we watch it or not. We like a lively background."

A girl in her mid-twenties says: "I suppose you would consider my family — four adults and four children living in a 600 square foot flat — to be pretty crowded.

A housing area in Wong Tai Sin. The most modern blocks are at the back.

But everything can be organized. Sleeping in a bunk bed is quite fun when you're very small. It's when you reach your teens that you start thinking about privacy."

Grandmother insists on maintaining a small shrine near the entrance door, and makes monthly offerings. But the real centre of family life is the table in the centre of the living room. The table is the meeting place for meals, for homework, for discussions, for mah-jong parties and, at times of disharmony, family quarrels.

"So much depends on relationships within the family," said a girl in her late teens. "You have got to be nice to each other — it's as simple as that. What if family members each want to watch a different TV programme? We often decide it by playing that game with fingers — you know, cloth, scissors, hammer. Or your mother's called in to decide. You'd be surprised how many disputes are settled by mother."

Dwellers in the older type of government flat can find lack of space irksome enough. " Too many people sharing one bathroom is an obstacle to the good life," says a middle-aged daughter, "and in times of water-rationing we have been utterly miserable. I remember those days when we had to put all our buckets and containers in line to make a queue to the standpipe, and there were nasty quarrels about who was in front. One day a horrid little boy put his dirty hands in the pail my sister had just filled, so she boxed his ears. Then his mother appeared and made a great fuss and hit my sister over the head with a bundle of vegetables. So then my sister poured the pail of water over her. Yet my sister is such a mild girl. It was all the discomfort and inconvenience of those awful summer days that started her off."

On the whole Hong Kong estate dwellers are a peaceable crowd. A young man speaks of the neighbourliness in government housing. The early H-blocks were not so good because the flats were back-to-back and you couldn't see your neighbours. Cooking had to be done on the balcony and the communal toilets were too often the scene of rape and robberies.

"But the more recent flats are very acceptable. You soon become ac-quainted with the family opposite and others along the corridor. In earlier days people who came to Hong Kong from different parts of Guangdong province

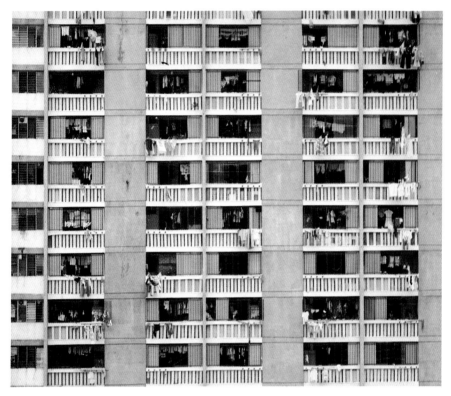

Sha Tin in Hong Kong's New Territories used to be a village between hills and the sea with a restaurant famous for roast pigeon. Now it's a huge New Town. Flats like these in the Wo Che Estate are well above average.

across the border, or from places further north like Shanghai, might be suspicious of each other, but things have changed enormously as a new generation grows up. Our parents are conscious of their roots but as for us younger people — we're Hong Kongers, and that's it. The origin of a friend's family doesn't much matter."

Estate dwellings bring their aesthetic limitations. "Not much opportunity for anything like creative activity," says one would-be artist. "Even if you managed to paint something, you may not be able to see it on a wall, to have a good look at it. Mother and father decide what goes on the walls."

One wardrobe has to accommodate all the family's clothes. One strip neon lighting serves the whole flat; that can make homework difficult for school children. Then shift work can bring its problems. "We come back from our

Spaces between housing blocks are well equipped for games. But mothers' fears of teenage Triads keeps some of the children away.

jobs at different hours of the night," says one young technician seeking new qualifications. "You don't want to disturb others by switching on at midnight. You can switch on a small lamp after midnight but somehow it's hard to do any work with people asleep all around you."

Happiness and security depend enormously on the bonds (or lack of them) between parents and children. Middle class Hong Kong has been horrified by the practice of leaving children locked up in the home while both parents go out to work. There was even a move last year to make this a punishable offence. However inquiries showed that although parents may leave children alone they don't generally do so willingly, out of greed and materialism, but simply because the two-parent income is a sheer necessity for keeping the family going.

Life in Hong Kong is far from cheap for those at the bottom end of the wages scale (three thousand two hundred a month), especially with all the fares to pay if home is far from the school or the place of work.

A new housing estate at Tai Po has a small but well laid out park area, as well as shops and restaurants.

Until now it's been the usual custom for young people to live with the family until they married. This still prevails in many families but in the last few years it has become easier for friends among the rising generation to share a flat on their own, though they won't qualify for government accommodation.

Just about forty-eight per cent of all Hong Kong people live in government housing estates, paying in rent far less than a fifth of their income, which is the norm set by United Nations guidelines. Estate living means you can save money, or invest in hi-fi equipment, TV, smart clothes. The government housing policy plays an important part in keeping Hong Kong people reasonably contented.

Mutual Aid Committees have been encouraged to develop further an atmosphere of good-neighbourliness. They vary in efficiency. Sometimes they are good at organizing social events, including snake banquets where every tenant chips in with seventy dollars or more. Some do good work in liaising with housing officers over tenants' complaints, especially faults in building leading to leaks and drainage problems.

They have even acted as organizers of vigilante groups when criminals are on the prowl; but on occasion they have shown themselves to be little better than Triads themselves, exacting contributions from tenants with little or nothing to show at the end of it.

Triads infiltrate everywhere. Count yourself lucky if you've never been contacted and know nothing about them. If your children "never go with bad people", that's also a cause for relief. But to make quite sure, you don't let your children play down below in the playground unless an older person is in charge of them.

A doctor concerned with social work remarked on the healthier appearance of children living in some of the shanty towns. "They're down there on ground level, they run about in the sunlight and enjoy plenty of freedom. Then the lucky day comes for the family to move into a government housing estate and soon these kids are living fifteen floors up and rarely get out except for school, and they look quite sickly." However no one who has moved out of a typical squatter area into government housing ever wants to return to life in a hut. "Your own bathroom, your own water tap, privacy, no protection to pay — until you experience this yourself you've no idea how well-off you are in government housing," says the mother of a family. "Of course it's cramped to some extent, but so is accommodation in the private sector at five times the price; and there you may have some unpleasant landlady who won't let you cook in the living room and rips you off for the electric light. Tougher still is life on a junk. All the people living on the water have the same ambition — to live on land."

The people who find Hong Kong living the hardest of all, however, are to be found among the seventy-five legal immigrants from Mainland China allowed into Hong Kong every day. You may say these immigrants are the lucky ones — they come armed with exit permits, able to start a new life. Many of them are wives joining their husbands or children reunited with parents.

"But it's by no means always a rosy picture," a social worker says. "To begin with about half of these newcomers come from more distant provinces and can't speak a word of Cantonese, and they're faced straight-

The art of living in confined space. Everyone has to behave in a considerate, civilized way; then life is more than tolerable. Harmony is everything.

away with the problem of somewhere to live. Of course they have no claim on government housing and the best available is a very small room costing Hong Kong $2,000 a month with water and electricity extra. It's usually partitioned off as part of a bigger room and so there's no window. How does a young couple with small children manage? They must get work straightaway and that isn't going to be easy if they don't speak Cantoneses; and they will have to find somewhere to leave the children. If they have relatives in Hong Kong, that may ease the burden, and a voluntary organization like International Social Service will try to help make contact with factories, get children into day nurseries or schools and organize language classes."

So the first year in Hong Kong is likely to be tough indeed. There are many disappointments. "Ignorance of Hong Kong conditions on the part of Main-landers is downright astonishing," says a Social Welfare official. "One thing the Mainland doesn't suffer from is lack of space. In the villages people are used to living in houses and they are deeply shocked when they find that two adults and three children may have to live in three hundred square feet. It's a major cause of family disputes and marriage break-ups."

Chapter 23

All Will Be Well — More or Less

The people of Hong Kong work, wait and watch while 30 June 1997 — the fateful day of hand-over — moves ever nearer.

Forecasts range from the positive to the complacent to the pessimistic. So many factors are involved that no predictions can be reliable.

As in the past Hong Kong's policies and daily life will be influenced by attitudes across the border, by the way Beijing looks at Hong Kong and the people here. At present, as everyone knows, the atmosphere is one of deep distrust — of fear that Britain may still try to retain influence even after the hand-over, concern that democratic influences may pose a threat to Chinese Mainland authority, that Governor Chris Patten has tried to make Hong Kong a subject of international concern and weaken Beijing's control.

Could this distrust evaporate after 1997 when the British have gone? Will Deng Xiaoping, now eighty-nine, still be a dominating voice in China? And when he quits the stage, will his death be followed by an intense power-struggle in Beijing? This has usually been the course of events when past leaders have died. And how would such a power-struggle affect Hong Kong?

What is really happening now in China? Although many people are immeasurably better-off, growing inequality is causing discontent. Yet to measure the political force of such discontent is virtually impossible because of the size and variety of China's provinces and the many differences in conditions of farmers, soldiers, city-workers, and the millions of unemployed.

You will hear Hong Kong businessmen say, never mind the inequalities, China is on the way to becoming a great economic power and a land of prosperity, and this process is irreversible, because so many powerful interests, in China and outside, are heavily involved. So the future is bright, and we do not need Mr Patten and his five-minutes-to-midnight electoral proposals; they only upset Beijing and cause us trouble.

This is not the view of many Hong Kong people, especially those under forty. They back the Governor, hoping that a bigger say in running their affairs will give them the chance to speak up and argue in defence of the freedoms promised them in the Joint Declaration.

Whatever happens, despite the brain-drain and the hostility of Beijing, the mass of Hong Kong people will still be there after 1997. Hong Kong, with its harbour and container-wharves, will still be a great trading port and China's window on the world. And the Hong Kong people will react to their new political environment as Chinese people have always done — hope for the best but be prepared for the not-so-good; and by hard work, luck and a strong family spirit, ensure survival and a life worth living.